— ❧ —

Maurice Burrell's *Preparing to Preach* draws upon years of preaching and teaching experience in churches of different denominations; in hospitals, colleges, and schools; as a chaplain with the British Forces in Germany; and more recently as director of education, and then of training, in the Diocese of Norwich.

He studied Theology at Bristol University, has a doctorate from Lancaster University, and has written books on fringe groups on the Christian perimeter.

His working class background, his strong family life and running nineteen marathons for charities have helped to keep his feet firmly on the ground. All of this has helped to equip him to produce a book that will help preachers who wish to meet the needs of the people who hear them.

PREPARING TO PREACH
A Handbook for Preachers

PREPARING TO PREACH
A Handbook for Preachers

Maurice Burrell

ATHENA PRESS
LONDON

ISBN 1 84401 446 0

First Published 2005 by
ATHENA PRESS
Queen's House, 2 Holly Road
Twickenham TW1 4EG
United Kingdom

Printed for Athena Press

Many thanks to Timothy Burrell for designing the cover

PREFACE

I wish to pay tribute to the many past preachers from whom I learned much. Two years before I began my ordination training, I discovered in a Free Church pastor named Ninian Lowis an excellent preacher with a rare gift for expository preaching. Percy Smith, the indefatigable Rector of St Augustine's Church, Norwich, where I grew up, gave me my first preaching opportunities and taught me much about the common touch in preaching. During my initial training for ordination, J Stafford Wright, Principal of what was to become Trinity College, Bristol, taught me to express the Christian faith thoughtfully and in clear and precise language.

I am grateful to the many people with whom I have worked throughout my ministry. In particular, during my time as Director of Education and then Director of Training in the Diocese of Norwich, I learnt much from teachers, colleagues and students, and am grateful to them all.

I owe much to my wife Sheila, who hears and comments on my sermons before I preach them, who encouraged me to complete this book, and who, as each chapter took shape, suggested how it might be improved.

Like all Christian disciples, I am still learning and never cease to wonder at the grace of God, who has entrusted the preaching of the Gospel of his Kingdom to fallible human beings like me. My prayer is that *Preparing to Preach* may encourage its readers in this most privileged ministry – that of preaching the Word of God.

Maurice Burrell
April 2005
Norwich

CONTENTS

INTRODUCTION

Many books have been written about preaching. David Buttrick's *Homiletic: Moves and Structures* and John Stott's *I Believe in Preaching* are two excellent attempts to cover the subject in detail. Three collections of sermons, Colin Gunton's *Theology through Preaching*, Rowan Williams' *Open to Judgement*, and John Bell's *Wrestle and Fight and Pray*, provide good examples of what it means to preach theologically and, at the same time, to preach in ways that relate to the life, work and witness of the Church. Publications from the College of Preachers have made their own significant contributions.

The traditions within the Christian Church from which these authors originate is significant. Professor Buttrick describes himself as a Protestant of the Reformed Tradition whose academic career has included seven years in a Catholic school of theology and visiting professorships with Baptists and the Disciples of Christ, as well as fourteen years in a Presbyterian seminary. John Stott is an internationally renowned representative of the evangelical wing of the Church of England whose preaching and teaching career has spanned most other denominations. Colin Gunton, who died whilst this book was being written, was a minister of the United Reformed Church and Professor of Christian Doctrine at King's College London. Rowan Williams was Lady Margaret Professor in Divinity at Oxford and is now Archbishop of Canterbury. Representing such a wide spectrum within the Church, they are a timely reminder that the ministry of God's Word can never be imprisoned within denominational boundaries.

Against that illustrious ecumenical background, it should cause no surprise that there is nothing specifically denominational about this book's contents. As its Church of England author, I received a broad-based, ecumenical initial theological training at Bristol University, where the theological faculty then consisted of the staff of five colleges, two of which were Anglican, one Methodist, one Congregational, and one Baptist. I am also married to a member of the United Reformed Church. It was inevitable, therefore, that something of the traditions of these and other denominations, for many of which I have preached, should rub off on me!

With so many excellent books like those mentioned above readily available, it might be asked why I have written yet another. The reason is simple. As seen in its title, this book seeks to fulfil a single purpose – to help its readers to become effective or more effective preachers. Focusing sharply on this single aim, *Preparing to Preach* deals with what may be called 'the nuts and bolts' of the preacher's preparation, which I believe is one of the most neglected areas in ordination and lay training.

Accordingly, I have written with three groups in mind: those at the beginning of their training for ordained or lay ministry in any of the Christian Churches; those recently ordained or licensed or accredited lay ministers faced with the problem of how best to use their limited time to prepare for their preaching; and experienced preachers, who may find it useful as a checklist against which to measure their own well-used methods. A problem which all preachers face is that their pastoral and other church commitments, their family responsibilities and their daily work, particularly if they are still in secular employment, make it difficult to give sermon preparation the priority it requires.

Preparing to Preach has been written from my experience of preaching in a variety of situations: in rural and urban parishes; in school, hospital, and college chapels; with the British Forces in Germany; and as director of training in the Diocese of Norwich. I have not presented a carefully argued apologia for, or a detailed theology of, preaching. I fully recognise the importance of both and my theological presuppositions will become clear to those who read on.

Many have written about the need for preachers to be dedicated to their task, urging them to give attention to their calling, their study of the Bible and theology, their character, and their spirituality. These are rightfully regarded as essential requirements of all preachers. The specific aim of this book is to help preachers to become effective or more effective preachers, so it is assumed that as they prepare to preach they will share five fundamental assumptions.

CALLING

Those preparing to preach either believe that God has called them to preach or are exploring whether they have such a vocation. The primary vocation shared by all Christians is that to Christian discipleship. This calling involves sharing in ministry in the general sense of serving God as they serve each other through the Church and in the world. The wide-ranging nature of that ministry is indicated in some of the New Testament's lists, notably by Paul in Romans 12 and 1 Corinthians 12. Although all are called to that all-embracing ministry, they are not all called to an identical share in that ministry. Those who believe they are called to preach need to undertake whatever training is necessary to develop their preaching skills. Then they have to test their vocation through their church to see whether it is willing to authorise them to exercise such a ministry.

COMMITMENT

Those called to the ministry of the Word are committed to *preaching*, not simply to the giving of short talks or longer addresses on religious topics, or even the telling of their faith story as an act of testimony. Talks, addresses and testimonies are important, not least as the means by which members of church congregations may be encouraged to share their faith and complement the work of preachers. Preaching, however, involves not occasional one-off contributions but an ongoing ministry of the Word.

As a traditional method of communicating the Christian faith, preaching has attracted much criticism, and not a little ridicule, in recent years. We are told that people have lost the ability to listen, and that when they do listen they want to hear informal, spontaneous, 'from the heart' contributions, rather than prepared set pieces. Critics remind preachers that people have been conditioned by television to expect far fewer words, spoken by a variety of people, interspersed with many pictures. They argue that the sermon is outdated and must give way to more effective methods of communication.

Those preparing to preach must not ignore the remarkable twentieth-century revolution in all branches of communication. There is much to learn from such developments. That having been said, preachers have no reason to believe that their role is outdated. They can be more optimistic than their critics and retain their faith in the relevance of preaching for today. Nevertheless all who preach have to remember that commitment to preaching also carries with it a commitment to the hard work of sermon preparation. Some experienced preachers have argued that this often means spending as much as an hour preparing for every minute they spend in the pulpit. Although this may seem too idealistic a target for busy preachers, it underlines the priority that needs to be given to sermon preparation.

STUDY

Those called to preach must also be willing to study. Sangster used to urge preachers to spend hours each day studying the Bible and reading theology. Today full-time ministers would argue that this high ideal is impossible in their busy lives when other demands, not least the pastoral needs of congregations, compete for their time and attention. Many lay preachers in secular employment or caring for families also have other commitments. Nevertheless, the fact cannot be avoided that every preacher needs to be a theologian. They may be good, bad, or modest theologians, but they can never escape their responsibility to keep their theology as up to date as they can.

Emphasising this essential link of theology and preaching, Christolph Schwobel writes,

> Because preaching is rooted in the communication of the triune God with his creation there is a close connection between preaching and theology [for] preaching non-theologically would be a contradiction in terms. Christian theology, which literally means reasonable discourse about God, is bound to preaching, because the Christian message is first of all gospel, the proclamation of the good news of God's grace in Christ. [Therefore,] preaching functions as a focus for the different aspects of theological competence; it brings together biblical interpretation, insight into the history of the church, doctrinal reflection and the considerations from practical theology about what makes a good sermon.[1]

---

[1] From Schwobel's Introduction to Gunton's *Theology Through Preaching*, p.4.

Clearly there is a sense then in which all preaching should be biblical preaching; for sermons attempt to point to the God who has revealed himself in Christ, the Incarnate Word, through the Bible, God's written word. If that is but an inkling of what preaching is meant to be, then clearly every preacher needs a good working knowledge of the Bible and of the Christian doctrine to which it has given rise. Without these, preaching will be at best without substance and at worst unchristian. Those who believe God has called them to preach need to equip themselves for this task for their own benefit and for the good of those who hear them.

CHARACTER

Preachers must also recognise the importance of what they *are* as well as what they *say*. They will wish to resist all attempts to set themselves up on pedestals, knowing that like all disciples they are fallible human beings who will never fully achieve those high ideals about which they preach. Yet the fact is that those listening to preachers expect them to exemplify to some degree the message they proclaim. Preachers must let their actions match their words by practising what they preach.

SPIRITUALITY

All preachers need to prepare themselves spiritually for their task, remembering that their ministry requires prayerfulness, humility, and a sense of privilege and responsibility. *Preparing to Preach* is based on the belief that God will have spoken first to the preacher before he speaks through the preacher to the congregation. This makes sermon preparation a personal spiritual experience as well as a practical piece of work.

These are five important presuppositions upon which

everything else in this book depends.

What follows is certainly not the only way to prepare to preach: it is my way. Others will do it differently and just as effectively. What is certain is that every preacher needs to develop a method of sermon preparation that works for him or her. All I can claim is that for many years the method set out in *Preparing to Preach* has worked for me. My hope is that it – or something like it – will work for you.

1. PREACHING ROLES

Dictionaries define preachers as those who deliver sermons or religious addresses; or, in a less complimentary way, as those who give moral advice, sometimes in an offensive, tedious or officious manner. Sermons are described as discourses, especially those delivered from pulpits, on a biblical text; or as harangues, reproofs, or moralising lectures. If these definitions reflect the popular perception of preachers and their sermons, it is not surprising that such a method of communication is often discredited, ignored and ridiculed. It is unfortunately true that some preaching may be offensive, can be obtrusive, and sometimes is tedious, but preaching is not merely the giving of an address or the offering of moral advice.

Those who have given their lives to the business of preaching have a more positive view. Sangster described preaching simply as 'a man speaking from God' and more profoundly as 'a manifestation of the Incarnate Word, from the Written Word, by the spoken word'.[2] John Stott, a contemporary preacher of international repute, says, 'Christianity is, in its very essence, a religion of the Word of God. No attempt to understand Christianity can succeed which overlooks or denies the truth that the living God has taken the initiative to reveal himself savingly to fallen humanity; or that his self-revelation has been given by the most straightforward means of communication known to us, namely by a word and words; or that he calls upon those who have heard his Word to speak it to others.'[3]

Behind such definitions of preaching lie the theological

---

[2] W E Sangster, *The Craft of Sermon Construction*, p.4.

[3] John Stott, *I Believe in Preaching*, p.15.

truths stated in the opening words of the Fourth Gospel. The Word who was 'with God' and 'was God', 'became flesh and lived among us'. So, although 'no one has ever seen God, it is God, the only Son … who has made him known'.[4] The first chapter of John's First Epistle develops this idea, indicating that the words of the apostles' message spring directly from their experience of that incarnate 'word of life', which they have heard, seen and handled in Christ.[5]

Elsewhere, Paul states, 'Faith comes from what is heard, and what is heard comes through the word of Christ.'[6] Christolph Schwobel comments, 'This points to the fact that in Christianity communication by words and signs is the paradigm for the relationship with God. God relates to us by addressing us and we are called to respond to this address.' For Schwobel, therefore, preaching is 'where the word of God becomes audible in human words about God'.[7]

Clearly, Schwobel, Sangster and Stott have a much higher view of preaching than that suggested by those dictionary definitions. Most experienced preachers would be equally positive. Many would argue that at the very least there is a different feel between giving addresses and preaching sermons. Modestly, they might fight shy of using Sangster's words of their own preaching, but they would agree in principle that, despite all their inadequacies, preachers are people speaking for God.

People speaking for God is a useful summary of the New Testament's view of preaching. Consider some of the ways its writers make clear this point with the titles they use to describe preachers.

---

[4] John 1:1, 14 and 18.
[5] 1 John 1:1–4.
[6] Romans 10:17.
[7] Schwobel's Introduction, in Colin Gunton's *Theology Through Preaching*, p.1.

HERALDS

Jesus, we are told, spent time in Galilee teaching in the synagogues and *proclaiming* the Gospel of the Kingdom,[8] and that later he chose the twelve to be with him and to be sent out to *preach*.[9] The Greek word used in these passages points to the ancient 'herald' whose duty was to make public proclamations – important in a preliterate society – shouting aloud what his superior wanted to be made known. The Christian preacher came to be seen, therefore, as a herald, a messenger from God, whose task was to proclaim the Good News of the Kingdom. Following in that great tradition, today's preachers may rightly be described as heralds. Their task is to make known God's truth that 'there is one God, and there is one mediator between God and man, Christ Jesus, himself man, who sacrificed himself to win freedom for all mankind'.[10]

SOWERS

Jesus is the sower in the parable of that name, and the four kinds of soil represent the responses from those who listen to his preaching:[11] some reject his teaching, some at first are impressed but in the longer term lack perseverance, some let material concerns crowd out his teaching, and some welcome his teaching and allow it to produce fruit in their lives. The parable makes it clear that Jesus was aware of this sowing role in his own ministry. Similarly, writing to a church founded as a result of his missionary activities but later split by factions, Paul reminded his readers that although he had planted the

---

[8] Matthew 9:35.
[9] Matthew 10:7.
[10] 1 Timothy 2:5.
[11] Mark 4:1–9.

seed and Apollos had watered it, it was God who produced the growth.[12]

The application of such teaching to contemporary preaching is clear. Fulfilling their role as sowers, preachers are fellow-workers with God, as well as with each other. They speak in God's name and know that without his blessing all their preaching will be ineffective. With a sense of privilege and humility, preachers do the work of sowers, recognising that as it was with Paul and Apollos then, so it is with them now. They 'broadcast' the seed of God's word, trusting God to produce fruit in the lives of those to whom they minister.

AMBASSADORS

Ambassadors are diplomats sent to represent their sovereign or state in another country. As official messengers they speak not for themselves but for their government. Similarly, as Paul implies in 2 Corinthians 5:20, preachers are Christ's ambassadors, people speaking for God. God has entrusted to all preachers the unique Christian 'ministry of reconciliation'. At the heart of their message lies the truth that 'God was in Christ reconciling the world to himself, not counting their trespasses against them'.[13] Exercising their ambassadorial role, they represent their King, appealing to their hearers to be reconciled to God through Christ.

STEWARDS

The writer of 1 Peter urges Christian disciples to be 'good stewards of the manifold grace of God' and in that context tells preachers to speak as those speaking the very words of God.[14] Similarly Paul describes himself and his fellow

---

[12] 1 Corinthians 3:6.
[13] 2 Corinthians 5:19.
[14] 1 Peter 4:10.

messengers as 'stewards of God's mysteries'.[15] Although the New Testament concept of stewardship applies to all Christians and to a range of activities much wider than speaking, in these two passages it has a particular reference to preachers. Preachers are stewards to whom God has delegated this particular form of Christian service and who are accountable to him for the way they exercise that ministry.

PROPHETS

The biblical prophets were primarily people of the word of God. The Lord called the Old Testament prophets to proclaim and interpret the word they had received from him. They introduced much of what they said with a phrase like, 'Thus said the Lord'.[16] They had an inner constraint to pass on to others what the Lord had first said to them. Primarily, they were *forth-tellers*, rather than fore-tellers. New Testament prophets inherited that great tradition. Timothy, for example, was told to fulfil his prophetic gift in preaching and teaching,[17] and Judas and Silas in exhorting and strengthening disciples.[18] Paul said that the task of prophets was to speak in such a way as to build up, encourage and console their fellow-disciples.[19] Contemporary preachers have a similar prophetic ministry. They may be used sometimes to bring new insights to the Church, yet are not the source of new truth. Rather, they proclaim, expound, interpret, and apply the Christian Gospel to their contemporary situation, or, as the letter to Jude put it, they 'contend for the faith that was once for all

---

[15] 1 Corinthians 4:1.
[16] Jeremiah 19:1, et al.
[17] 1 Timothy 4:14.
[18] Acts 15:32.
[19] 1 Corinthians 14:3.

entrusted to the saints'.[20] In that sense, all preachers are prophets.

ENABLERS

This word does not appear in the New Testament but the idea behind 'enablers' is clearly expressed in Ephesians 4. Church leaders, that is apostles, prophets, evangelists, and pastor-teachers, are called to exercise their particular ministry by equipping other disciples for their ministries. They do this by 'building up the body of Christ', thus contributing to the growth towards maturity in Christ which must be the aim of all disciples.[21] In that New Testament tradition, preachers are to be enablers, equipping and empowering all church members for their ministry within the Church and to the world that all Christians share. With current anxiety in all branches of the Church about difficulties of meeting increasing costs of stipendiary ministers, accompanied by calls for an urgent rethink of ministerial strategies, the enabling role of unpaid ministry offered by many lay people is vital.

EVANGELISTS

According to the earliest of the Gospels, 'Jesus came into Galilee, proclaiming the good news of God'.[22] 'Good news' is a translation of a Greek word *euangelion* from which we derive the word 'evangelist'. Mark goes on to record that Jesus told Simon and Andrew, 'Follow me and I will make you fish for people.'[23] The Twelve were later called as Christ's apostles 'to be with him, and to be sent out to proclaim the

---

[20] Jude 3.
[21] Ephesians 4:11–12.
[22] Mark 1:14.
[23] Mark 1:17.

message',[24] and were sent out to proclaim the Good News, that is, to evangelise. All Christian preachers are called to proclaim that same gospel. Some preachers, together with many others who are not called to preach, have a specific gift for evangelism. For this reason and others, not least the fact that much evangelism takes place as individual Christians share their faith with people they contact outside church buildings, evangelism cannot be the sole preserve of public preachers. Nevertheless, because of their responsible and privileged role and the opportunities given them to preach the Good News of the Kingdom, they cannot escape their evangelistic role.

PASTOR-TEACHERS

Pastor-teachers figure prominently in the list of those Christian leaders in Ephesians 4:11 called to exercise their own ministry by equipping other disciples for their ministry. Whilst the distinctive role of pastors is to care for the flock, that of teachers is to pass on the Christian tradition. In Ephesians 4, however, pastors and teachers seem to be brought together into a single office, that of pastor-teachers. Although nowadays pastors and teachers are sometimes thought to belong to two distinct categories of ministry, thought to be endowed with different gifts, and called to exercise distinctive roles, that view can be pressed too far. Pastors and teachers belong together and need each other. Moreover, in reality the same person often exercises the two roles within a church fellowship. The writer of Ephesians 4 seems to believe that, ideally, that is how it should be.

Charles Smyth was convinced about the importance of the link between the two roles. Fifty years ago he argued

---

[24] Mark 3:14.

that preaching was in itself a pastoral activity and that people could not preach God's Word with power if they were 'isolated from the rough and tumble of a pastoral ministry'.[25] In his day, most of the preaching in most denominations was still done by ordained stipendiary ministers and they were expected to exercise both a preaching and a pastoral ministry. The last twenty-five years has been marked by a steady decline in the number of stipendiary ministers, the blossoming of non-stipendiary ordained ministry, and the increase of lay involvement in ministry of all kinds.

Because of such developments, many of those who now preach regularly have no formal pastoral responsibilities. This makes it all the more essential for all preachers to remember that there is a close relationship between the pastoral and the teaching roles. On the one hand, those who believe their strength lies in teaching, need to develop pastoral insights to make sure that their teaching is earthed in reality and thus relevant to those who hear them. On the other hand, those who feel much more at home as pastoral carers, will wish to look to the teaching enshrined in the Christian tradition to motivate and monitor this aspect of their ministry.

STORYTELLERS

Jesus enlightened his listeners by presenting them with truths illustrated from the everyday life with which they were familiar. 'Without a parable he told them nothing.'[26] He then left them to perceive and apply those truths to themselves. Sometimes his parables were short, pithy sayings, like, 'Why do you look at the speck in your neighbour's eye, but do not notice the log in your own

---

[25]. Charles Smyth, *The Art of Preaching: 947 to 1939.*
[26] Matthew 13:34.

eye?'[27] Often they were longer stories, such as the well-known parables of the lost son, the lost sheep, or the lost coin in Luke 15.

This well-tried teaching method, with its long and successful Middle-East track record, has not outlived its usefulness, particularly in a post-Christian era where there is widespread ignorance about the Christian message. Because it can no longer be taken for granted that people are familiar with basic Christian teaching, the importance of preachers as storytellers cannot be exaggerated. The central Christian story of Christ's coming, living, dying, and rising, especially needs to be as much at the heart of 21st-century preaching as it was in the first-century Church. Following our Master's example, preachers can use the art of storytelling to win people's attention, to stimulate their thinking, to dispel their ignorance, and to encourage them to see the relevance of the Gospel to their lives today, and to make their response.

ADVOCATES

Secular advocates plead the cause of their clients in law courts. The New Testament makes use of this metaphor in the Fourth Gospel and John's First Letter, describing both Jesus and the Holy Spirit as advocates. Jesus pleads our cause with his Father,[28] and the Holy Spirit pleads God's cause with us.[29] Although the New Testament never applies the title 'advocate' to preachers, the implication is there. They too are advocates who plead God's cause with men and women. As they exercise that role, preachers can learn from the care with which secular advocates prepare and then argue with passion the cases of their clients in the law courts.

---

[27] Matthew 7:4.
[28] 1 John 2:1.
[29] John 14:25, 15:26, 16:7–11.

APOLOGISTS

These have a long and respectable history within the Christian Church from Paul onwards, for he acted as an apologist in his Areopagus sermon in Acts 17:23 when he tried to commend the truth of the resurrection to Greek philosophers. Recently, Alister McGrath has commended this apologistic approach in his book *Bridge Building*, arguing that 'apologetics aims to lend intellectual integrity and depth to evangelism, ensuring that faith remains rooted in the head, as well as in the heart'.[30] It is an emphasis that needs to be much more in evidence in contemporary attempts to communicate the Christian Gospel within a secular environment and, although apologetics cannot be limited to preaching, the two are closely linked. McGrath illustrates the relationship between the two from Paul's Areopagus sermon, saying that *kerygma* and *apologia* are two aspects of a greater whole. 'Both are essential components of the proclamation of Christ … to proclaim the gospel is to defend the gospel [and] to defend the gospel is to proclaim the gospel.'[31]

BUILDERS

Paul described the Corinthian Christians as 'God's building' and called himself and others whom God used to found and develop that Church as those building on the foundation of Jesus Christ.[32] 'Builders' is an apt description of the role of preachers. Sometimes preachers are called to be pioneer builders, those given the privilege of building from scratch, laying the foundations on 'bare building sites'. Most are more likely to find themselves building on foundations laid

---

[30] Alister McGrath, *Bridge Building*, p.9.
[31] Ibid., p.49.
[32] 1 Corinthians 3:9–10.

by earlier preachers, and often getting the credit which belonged to their predecessors.

Years ago I was part of a student mission team, which worked for just two weeks on a large urban council estate, during which a number of people committed themselves to the Christian faith. Two are full-time ministers. At the time, the youthful team received much of the credit for what had been a very successful mission. We all knew, however, that the exciting results we saw after our brief visit to the parish came about entirely because of the strong foundations painstakingly laid over several years by a hardworking vicar and his curate. We built on their foundations.

COMMUNICATORS

This communicating role of preachers is an obvious conclusion to a chapter dealing with preaching roles, for it is in effect a summing up of all those roles mentioned earlier. All preachers are meant to communicate. Unless we are communicating we are not preaching. What needs to be clear, however, is the sense in which we are communicators. We are not seeking only to inform and educate, important though these aspects of communication are. We are sharing good news, and helping people with us to discover in Christ the meaning of life. As we communicate in that wider sense, we are also revealing to those who hear us something of ourselves, our hopes and our aspirations. We cannot do that merely by enunciating facts or giving information in an objective way. We speak *from the heart* about matters that concern us and which we hope to persuade others to share with us. All the other preaching roles mentioned earlier have something to contribute to our work as preachers.

Clearly no preacher, no matter how gifted, can be a perfect communicator: none of us can fulfil all the roles of herald, sower, ambassador, steward, prophet, enabler, evangelist, pastor-teacher, storyteller, advocate, apologist and builder. Sometimes we have to decide which of those roles we shall occupy on specific occasions. More often we shall discover that one or more roles come into play in our preaching. Always our personality, temperament and gifts will also help to determine which of these roles come most naturally to us.

To avoid getting into a rut, however, it is helpful from time to time to remind ourselves of the wide variety of preaching roles, especially when we are preaching to the same congregations week after week. We owe it to our congregations to avoid being entirely predictable.

When all has been said, however, we all have our strengths and weaknesses. We need to remember, therefore, that God graciously uses us as we are. We are preachers, 'people speaking from God'. More profoundly our preaching is meant to be 'a manifestation of the Incarnate Word, from the Written Word, by the spoken word'.[33] As Christians we believe that God himself is the perfect Communicator. Therein lies our motivation and the strength we need as despite all our inadequacies we seek to communicate for Him.

---

[33] Sangster, op. cit., p.4.

2. PREACHING STYLES

Members of our congregations are unlikely to know of, or care about, what some pundits call sermon classification. Ask any who attend church about their preacher's style or the type of sermon preached and their reply is likely to be brief and to the point. Their sermon classification is based on some simple criteria, expressed in their answers to a few fairly basic questions. Did the preacher communicate? Was the preacher on the right wavelength? Was the sermon short or long, interesting or boring, memorable or forgettable, relevant or irrelevant, simplistic or thought-provoking? Did they believe that God was speaking to them through the preacher's words?

These are the kind of questions preachers should constantly ask themselves, for congregations describe preaching by the impact it makes upon them. Nevertheless, for preachers themselves a more sophisticated form of sermon classification is an important tool, which when used carefully may help to develop the skills needed to make preaching more consumer-friendly.

Probably the most careful analysis of preaching remains that made by W E Sangster half a century ago.[34] Sangster classified sermons according to their subject matter, the psychological stance of their preachers, and the structural organisation of their content. As we shall see, within each of these main areas he set out a number of subcategories. Although Sangster's analysis is still a useful foundation upon which to build, it needs to be revised to take account

---

[34] W E Sangster, *The Craft of Sermon Construction*.

of the revolution in communication skills of recent years.

Style is my word for what Sangster described as *preachers' psychological stances.* In essence he meant the methods or techniques preachers adopt, what might be called their modus operandi. Preachers do not consistently use the same style, often varying their styles on different occasions and for different purposes. Sangster's classification lists four such stances or styles, which he calls authoritative, persuasive, cooperative, or subversive. My preferred descriptions are direct, interactive, narrative, and multimedia styles; and I have given three of these main styles their own sub-styles, as demonstrated below.

Although most preachers might adopt preaching styles unconsciously, it may be helpful to look at them in some detail for two reasons. First, there is an obvious connection between styles and some of the preaching roles examined in Chapter 1. Secondly, some conscious attention to styles may help to make our preaching more varied and so more interesting.

DIRECT	INTERACTIVE	NARRATIVE	MULTIMEDIA
Prophetic	Conversational	Storytelling	
Didactic	Cooperative	Account giving	
Dialectic			
Subversive			
Persuasive			

DIRECT PREACHING

The adjective 'direct' describes preachers whose characteristic preaching style is straightforward, explicit, and immediate. These are the kind of preachers who say what they mean, and mean what they say. Their preaching is without frills, and gets to the point as quickly as possible. They rarely employ the more involved, sophisticated, and – some would say – more leisurely approaches of the interactive, narrative, and multimedia styles.

The direct style usually takes the form of a monologue, using 'monologue' in the non-pejorative sense of something spoken by one person and not in the pejorative sense of a tedious speech that blocks response. It perhaps best describes preaching in its traditional form. One person preaches and the congregation listens in silence. Though on rare occasions it has been known for a stage-managed heckler to bait a preacher to make a congregation sit up and take notice, this is unusual. Listeners do not normally behave in this manner, and are not encouraged to interrupt, ask questions, agree or disagree, enter into discussion, or articulate their response in any other way, while the sermon is being preached. The preacher's task is to speak: the congregation's part is to listen, and hopefully to respond silently in mind and heart to where the sermon is leading.

This, more than any other style, is the style of preaching that gives rise to one of the chief criticisms levelled against preaching today. Preachers, it is said, place themselves six feet above contradiction. As we shall see, there are other styles which take account of such feelings and attempt, not always successfully, to encourage congregational participation. Different styles suit different occasions and meet different needs. Despite the criticism it sometimes evokes, the direct style should not be set aside lightly. Not only has it a long and distinguished history, but it can still be very effective when used by a preacher who is properly prepared. A clear case can be made for claiming that it remains an appropriate style for a preacher to adopt for some sermons.

As illustrated in the diagram, there are five distinct, but closely related, categories of direct preaching.

PROPHETIC STYLE

Using the prophetic style, preachers are concerned to proclaim a divinely given message. They believe they are speaking for God. Because of this, prophetic preaching is often, though not exclusively, closely associated with biblical preaching, the use of the Bible helping to emphasise that the message is God's, not the preacher's.

Preaching of this style often has a strong evangelistic, moral or social application, and might develop such themes as *Inviting Christ into your life as Saviour and Lord*, *Gambling*, *Materialism*, *Our country's poor and homeless*, or *Africa's starving millions*. Characterised by an element of the Old Testament prophets' 'Thus says the Lord', it is usually clear and uncompromising. It often includes a direct and clear-cut challenge to individual hearers and communities to make a practical response to the message being proclaimed, such as, *Repent and believe the Gospel*, *Lobby your member of parliament*, *Support Shelter*, or *Help to raise money for Christian Aid, Cafod, Oxfam, or Tearfund*.

DIDACTIC STYLE

The aim of the preacher using the didactic style of preaching is to teach some aspect of Christian truth. The sermon's theme may be doctrinal: *What Christians believe about the Trinity*, or *What it means to be made in God's image*, or *Why Jesus died*. Equally, some didactic sermons may develop a devotional theme like, *Worshipping God in spirit and in truth*, or *What to expect when we come to Holy Communion*.

DIALECTIC STYLE

Using the dialectic style, preachers attempt to argue a case in support of some aspect of the Christian faith. They might, for example, pose the simple question, *Should Christians always tell the truth?* Or they might highlight a contemporary ethical issue about people being allowed to die with dignity, and from that might even move on to the arguments for and against euthanasia. The field in this style of preaching is very wide, but, whatever the subject, the preaching method is generally the same. Preachers present their material in a logical way, stating the case in favour of their proposition and seeking to demolish the arguments on the other side. Confident preachers will then leave their congregations to make up their own minds, less confident ones will try to make it up for them!

SUBVERSIVE STYLE

What some have called a subversive style provides an interesting, if somewhat risky, variation of the dialectic style's use of argument. With the subversive style, preachers argue the case *against* the truths they believe in and are trying to teach, but do so in such a way as to show that the case against does not hold water. Sangster, who occasionally used the subversive style, admitted that it required an experienced preacher and a sophisticated congregation, and should be used sparingly. He sometimes used it when preaching to students. Knowing how easily preachers can be misunderstood, even without the added obstacle of the subversive approach, some would say it should never be used.

PERSUASIVE STYLE

This is similar to the dialectic style – the advocacy of a case – but in practice it tends to be emotionally warmer. Whereas in the dialectic style preachers appeal to the head, in the persuasive style they appeal to the heart.

The strength of the persuasive style is that preachers are recognising the importance of feelings and involving people's emotions in the issues at stake, rather than allowing them to stand apart and consider them in some coldly aloof way. Conversely, its weakness is that the feelings may be stirred only temporarily: hearers may be persuaded to respond with warmth to an eloquent preacher, but when the emotions subside nothing remains. Such criticism has to be weighed against the equally strong argument that some other preaching styles have more in common with dry, remote and irrelevant academic lectures at one extreme, and cosy chats at the other.

Rational and emotional appeal both have their place: some may be convinced by the logic of mental processes; others will be moved by their feelings. Perhaps an ideal style is achieved when preachers are able to combine the two, convincing minds by sound argument and stirring hearts by their strength of feelings.

INTERACTIVE PREACHING

Whereas a direct style of preaching nearly always takes the form of a monologue, the interactive style is essentially a dialogue, vocal communication between two or more people. The intention of a preacher using the interactive style is to encourage some hearers, and sometimes whole congregations, to become actively involved in the preaching process. This style also has its sub-styles, the two most obvious being the conversational and the cooperative styles.

CONVERSATIONAL STYLE

This conversational style of preaching is in the form of a dialogue between at least two people. Although they can be imaginary conversations which preachers have with themselves in the presence of their congregations, more usually they are conversations between preachers and selected members of their congregations. One of their most popular forms is the interview, either with preachers directing well-prepared questions to the interviewees, who are equally well prepared with their answers. Or they can be less carefully rehearsed and therefore more spontaneous dialogues. This style is far less formal than the more direct styles of preaching considered earlier, and for that reason can often reach people who may react against the more authoritative, didactic, and reasoning styles. As a technique, it can often be seen operating at both its best and its worst on television.

COOPERATIVE STYLE

Cooperative preaching is really a further development of the conversational style, with two or more people working together to present the sermon material. In its simplest form, members of the congregation can be asked to read pre-arranged quotations to be used by the preachers. As television newsreader's show, some interplay between different voices can help to hold people's attention in a way not always true when one person is speaking at some length without a break.

The style can be developed further with a preacher trying to encourage a whole congregation to participate in the experience, not merely by some reading pre-arranged quotations, but by making their own comments or asking questions. Such congregational participation can be pre-arranged, with members being invited some time beforehand to participate. This has the added advantage that contributors can be carefully briefed, not least about the length of their contribution. On the other hand, spontaneous contributions may lead to a livelier sermon. Such an approach is not without risk, for it may provide open house for those who like the sound of their own voices, and it can degenerate into a general pooling of ignorance and prejudice. Handled well by an able leader, however, it has its place and can be very effective.

NARRATIVE PREACHING

A narrative style of preaching is one in which the preacher either tells a story or gives an account.

TELLING A STORY

The art of storytelling is as old as mankind, so it is hardly surprising that from the earthly ministry of Jesus onwards storytelling has had a distinguished track record as a successful method of conveying Christian truth. As a preaching style, it comes into its own particularly where congregations are of a mixed background, of wide age range, and at different stages in their Christian discipleship, for the story is capable of different levels of understanding and application. It can help fill gaps in the Bible knowledge of adults and children.

Storytelling should not be treated as an easy option, however, for preachers using it need to prepare as thoroughly as they would for any other kind of preaching. In particular, they need to be clear about when they will leave the story to speak for itself and when they will try to explain and apply its message. The example of Jesus shows that when the story is a strong one its hearers can usually be left to discover its meaning for themselves. Sometimes a story's impact can be ruined when the narrator tries to explain it. Though a preaching style in its own right, most preachers will probably find that telling a story is more helpful as *part* of a sermon, rather than as the whole sermon.

GIVING AN ACCOUNT

The narrative style can also take the form of the giving of an account, a style that is often very much in evidence when overseas mission visitors occupy the pulpit. Traditionally, their sermons consist of a string of short accounts illustrating aspects of their work, followed by attempts to encourage congregations to pray, give financial help, and provide other kinds of support. At best, such visitors are good examples of how the style can be used. At worst, they are salutary reminders of the weakness of sermons made up of a string of anecdotes which have not been properly prepared and have no unifying aim.

MULTIMEDIA PREACHING

This style has developed in response to the communication explosion of the last half-century. It acknowledges that churchgoers, like the rest of society, now have easy access to all kinds of information through broadcasting and computers, and have learnt to expect that information to come to them in user-friendly forms. Adapting to this technological revolution, the preacher becomes more of a presenter than a traditional preacher, using a variety of methods which may include films, video recordings, music, and pre-recorded interviews or extracts. The possibilities seem to be endless. An occasional presentation of this kind may be a welcome variation from more traditional preaching.

As with all forms of preaching, there are no short cuts. Schoolteachers and adult educators have long ago learnt that the use of modern communication methods, though very effective when their use is carefully planned, often make for more work not less. In the hands of those who have not taken the trouble to learn how modern technology operates and who see modern communication methods as ends rather than means, the multimedia style can be an embarrassment and, on occasions, counterproductive. Careful observation of how the best television presenters and interviewers operate, and the obvious professionalism they bring to their work, will show preachers wishing to adopt a multimedia style of preaching that they will have to work hard to communicate their message effectively.

STYLES AND ROLES

There are some obvious links between some of the preaching roles of Chapter 1 and some of the preaching styles of this chapter. Those preachers who regard themselves chiefly as exercising the roles of herald, ambassador, prophet, evangelist and advocate, may prefer the direct style as defined earlier. They prefer their preaching to be straightforward, explicit, and immediate, aim to say what they mean and mean what they say, and intend to preach without frills so they may get to the point of their proclamation as quickly as possible. Those who interpret their roles primarily as sower, steward, enabler, storyteller, and builder, may find themselves more at home using the interactive, narrative, and multimedia styles.

None of this is as clear-cut as it first appears. Take, for example, that crucial role of pastor-teachers. What, for example, is the preferred method of pastor-teachers? Is the approach to be formal, informal, or a blend of both? If we are formal, then our clear preference will be for a didactic style of direct preaching. If we prefer a more informal teaching method, then we may be more at ease with the conversational and cooperative styles of interactive preaching. And if we are the kind of people who see good in both formal and informal educational methods, then we shall probably work hard to achieve some kind of working balance between all kinds of methods. We shall not stop to ask ourselves whether our methods are formal or informal, but rather will they work – and especially will they work in this situation, with these people, at this time? As we do that, we shall almost certainly find ourselves employing both direct and interactive styles, and from time to time also the narrative and, perhaps, multimedia styles as well.

What is also clear is that preferred preaching styles are

often closely associated with preachers' personalities. Some preachers will feel happier using a forthright prophetic style. Others will be more comfortable with a relaxed conversational or storytelling style. Yet others will feel at home with modern communication technology. Preachers need to be themselves. Nevertheless, all preachers may find it helpful to be aware of, to cultivate, and from time to time to try out, preaching styles other than those which seem to come most naturally to them. What also needs to be borne in mind is that some preaching styles may be better suited than others to the presentation of a particular theme.

AUTHORITATIVE PREACHING

We have seen that Sangster, when classifying sermons according to the psychological stance adopted by their preachers, categorised them as authoritative, persuasive, cooperative, and subversive. He clearly believed that sermons preached in what we have called the direct style, especially when they involved expository preaching, were more authoritative than those that we have described as interactive, narrative, or multimedia styles. 'There are times when the note of authority is called for, and it is called for supremely in the proclamation of the Word of God. Proclaim it, therefore! Tell it out! Thus says the Lord...'[35]

Authoritative preaching, however, need not be limited to direct biblical exposition. Any style of preaching, used well, can be authoritative, whereas any style, including those in the direct style, when used badly can be anything but authoritative. An authoritative sermon is one that commands attention, rings true, and stimulates a response from its hearers, because they recognise it as an authentic word of God, a trustworthy testimony to God's truth. Using

---

[35] Ibid., p.101.

that definition, *every* sermon, whatever its preacher's style, should be authoritative.

Authoritative preaching must not be confused, however, with authoritarian preaching. The two are quite distinct. An *authoritarian* style has little or no respect for the individual, can be tyrannical and dictatorial, allows no views different from that of the preacher, and therefore recognises the legitimacy of no response but that of agreement. Authoritarian preachers are often hard, insensitive, frequently very loud, and lacking that proper sense of humility expected of those privileged to speak for God. On the other hand, authoritative preachers, though personally convinced of the truth of their message, will be ready to acknowledge the possibility that sometimes they may have got it wrong.

3. SERMON TYPES

The previous chapter dealt with 'styles', the particular stances a preacher adopts in preaching. Here we move on to 'types', the subject matter or contents of sermons.

Ask any group of preachers to list sermons according to their subject matter, and the end product is unlikely to spring many surprises. Their suggestions would probably fall into one or other of the categories shown in the following diagram. Any classification is bound to be subjective. Some would prefer more and others fewer main types, and in practice many sermons will not fit neatly into any one type so there will be overlaps. It will be seen that even with the seven main types below, it has been necessary to add to six of them three or more sub-types.

TYPES	SUB-TYPES		
Biblical	Single texts	Longer passages	Bible themes
Topical	Ethical	Social	Environmental
Discipleship	Means of grace	What to believe	How to live
Stewardship	The earth	Possessions and time	Gifts and service
Biographical	Bible characters	Historical characters	Contemporary characters
Outreach	Evangelistic	Apologetic	
Historical			

What needs to be stressed is that the classification of sermons according to their subject matter, or in any other way, is far from being an exact science. Nevertheless, the exercise is of value if it does nothing more than to encourage preachers to broaden their repertoire, for that may prevent staleness and stimulate the interest of congregations.

BIBLICAL SERMONS

The preachers of Nehemiah's time 'read from the book of the law of God clearly, made its sense plain, and gave instructions in what was read'.[36] They would have agreed with the Psalmist that the unfolding, opening up, and explanation of God's Word gives light.[37] Such expository preaching has been a fundamental part of Christian preaching from its beginning. Preaching is the spoken attempt to point to the God who has revealed himself in Christ, God's Incarnate Word, through the Bible, God's written word. Because preachers are called to proclaim God's word, it has been argued that 'no preaching out of harmony with the Bible, and no preaching which could not honestly be related to the Bible, can establish its claim to be Christian preaching'.[38] If all sermons should in that sense be biblical, what are the criteria for labelling some of them as specifically biblical?

A specifically biblical sermon is one which not only uses biblical material to develop its theme but one which focuses single-mindedly on a specific section of the biblical text, attempts to give a detailed explanation of it, and brings out its meaning and application to contemporary life. Some writers have classified such biblical preaching as either textual or

[36] Nehemiah 8:7ff.
[37] Psalm 119:130.
[38] W E Sangster, *The Craft of Sermon Construction*, p.25f.

45

expository. Though the difference between them is not always clear, those who maintain this distinction say that *textual* sermons are those which focus on one or, at the most, two Bible verses, whereas *expository* sermons usually handle longer sections of scripture. This seems an unnecessary complication, for in all biblical sermons preachers will wish to apply the skills of the biblical scholar to their subject matter, using the skills of exegesis to examine the critical issues raised by a particular passage and that of hermeneutics to interpret the passage in the light of its cultural and historical context. As shown in the table earlier, I have subdivided biblical preaching into sermons dealing with single texts, longer passages, and Bible themes.

SINGLE TEXTS

These are what many people understand by preaching, and some older members of congregations bemoan the fact that preachers seldom preach like this today. With some nostalgia they remember preachers who would announce their text at the beginning, refer to its context, explain its meaning, and lead on to its message for today. That, they tell us, was real preaching. It has its disadvantages. Few preachers who preach single text sermons would now start by announcing the text, recognising that usually they need to introduce their chosen verse in a way that will capture the congregation's attention and prepare the way for what the verse teaches. Some preachers fail to provide the exposition of scripture that the announcement of the text has promised, using it instead as a peg on which to hang a sermon which bears little relation to the text. Provided it is used sensibly and in a disciplined way, however, there is still value in this approach, for it focuses the congregation's attention on a manageable, and sometimes a memorable, Bible passage.

LONGER PASSAGES

These may range from a few verses to much longer sections of the Bible. So, for example, the sermon may focus on one of Isaiah's servant songs, one of the parables or miracles of Jesus, or an extract from a New Testament letter. During a service of Holy Communion a preacher might expound one of the set readings. More ambitiously, some preachers, rather than expound an isolated passage, will try to tackle a whole book. Where this is one of the shorter books like Philemon or 3 John, this may be realistic. Otherwise, preachers may feel that they must discipline themselves to work through successive sections of a chosen book week by week. One gifted London expository preacher worked steadily through Paul's letter to the Romans. Though it took him many months, large numbers attended regularly to benefit from his careful exposition. It should be noted, however, that his eclectic London congregation, who travelled miles to hear him, was not that of a typical local church.

BIBLE THEMES

Another approach to expository preaching is to tackle one of the great Bible themes such as creation, covenant, law, grace, sacrifice, atonement, faith, salvation, or resurrection. This kind of preaching helps people to see both the unity and the diversity of scripture, as well as the progressiveness of the God-given revelation. As with every other type of preaching, thematic preaching requires careful preparation, an appreciation of what is manageable in the time available, and a sensitive attempt to relate a particular theme to the needs and concerns of the congregation.

STRENGTHS AND WEAKNESSES

The potential weakness of such preaching is that, in the

wrong hands, it can sometimes become little more than a dry, detached, remote and irrelevant academic discussion of things which happened two thousand or more years ago, or the 'bible-bashing' technique which borders on indoctrination. Its strength, however, lies in the authority it derives from its strong biblical base. Preachers believe that they are not simply giving their personal views but are proclaiming God's Word.

TOPICAL SERMONS

The purpose behind topical preaching is not primarily to expound scripture but to explore contemporary ethical, social, and environmental concerns from a Christian point of view. The overlap between these three areas often make it almost impossible to place them tidily in these three sub-styles. There is a much clearer distinction between topical and biblical sermons, even though topical preachers will wish to use scripture in exploring topical issues.

Topical sermons will inevitably range widely over what can be a limitless field.

- *Ethical sermons* may attempt to deal with issues such as genetic engineering, sexual behaviour, euthanasia, and business standards.
- *Social sermons* may focus on matters of equal public concern like care for the elderly, education, housing, health, and the world of work.
- *Environmental sermons* may try to draw attention to the decline of some urban and rural communities, to the environmental costs of major road development across areas of natural beauty, and to the ever-present anxieties about environmental pollution.

Because the kind of issues explored in topical sermons often receive wide media coverage, preachers are encouraged to feel that they are not preaching in a vacuum, and that their congregations are made aware that current issues are being addressed from a Christian point of view.

STRENGTHS AND WEAKNESSES

The potential disadvantage of topical preaching is that it can be used as a platform for preachers who, with limited knowledge of the underlying issues of their topics, can make uninformed judgements about them. They also face the danger of airing prejudices without referring to any specifically biblical or generally Christian perspectives that may throw light on their chosen topics. Its obvious strength is the interest it engenders because it tries to address current, real life situations, matters that are of general concern to their hearers.

BRIDGE-BUILDING SERMONS

We have noted potential weaknesses in the types of preaching outlined so far. They include the possibility that those expounding the Bible may fail to apply scriptural teaching to the contemporary situation, and those addressing contemporary issues may neglect biblical and Christian perspectives on the issues they raise. Because of this, some see the need for a type of preaching which is not exclusively one or the other but both.

John Stott, for example, has advocated a bridge-building type of preaching. Whilst agreeing that all authentically Christian preaching must be biblical, he says that if preaching is no more than the interpretation of biblical documents it lacks contemporary application. The preacher has to relate the Bible's message to the existential situation. 'Preaching is not exposition only but communication, not just the exegesis of a text but the conveying of a God-given message to living people.'

'A bridge,' Stott continues, 'is a means of communication between two places which would otherwise be cut off from one another by a river or a ravine.' Similarly, there is a deep rift between the biblical and the modern worlds. Stott therefore advocates sermons which are truly expository but which also deal with contemporary ethical, social, and political issues. He wants sermons which are both biblical and topical.[39]

Though there is much to support Stott's view, it does not seem to necessitate another separate 'bridge-building' category. All preaching, however we label it, must make an honest attempt to proclaim and interpret what the Bible says, and also to show how biblical principles can be applied to contemporary issues. For the Bible is not an end in itself: 'All inspired scripture has its use for teaching the truth and refuting error, or for reformation of manners and discipline in right living' so that people may be equipped for good work of every kind.[40] All preachers need to be bridge-builders, especially when they are preaching outreach-type sermons which we shall consider later.

DISCIPLESHIP SERMONS

Whereas topical preaching latches onto issues of concern to contemporary society at large, this third type of preaching provides clear teaching on those matters which are of particular concern to the life of the Church corporately and to its members individually. Designed to help church members grow in their understanding of, and their commitment to, Christian discipleship, discipleship sermons may be considered as 'means of grace', 'what to believe' and 'how to live' sermons.

---

[39] John Stott, *I Believe in Preaching*, p.135ff.
[40] 2 Timothy 3:16–17.

MEANS OF GRACE

'Means of grace' sermons will focus on such matters as worship, prayer and the sacraments, those God-given means through which Christians are helped to grow in their discipleship. Because preachers are among those who, hopefully, are growing, they are likely to approach this kind of preaching with even more humility than usual. Like those to whom they preach, they are travelling: they have not yet arrived. Nevertheless, exercising their role as pastor-teachers, they must endeavour to provide whatever help they can for their fellow travellers.

Preachers may wish to explore with their congregations topics such as these: *What is worship? Is worship for God's benefit, or ours? How do worship, work and witness overlap? What do Christians believe they are doing when they pray? Is corporate prayer more effective than private prayer? Are there methods of prayer that need to be learnt? Is prayer always answered? Why is Holy Communion important? In what sense are the bread and wine Christ's body and blood? What does Baptism mean?*

WHAT TO BELIEVE

These are the sermons intended to help Christians explore what they profess to believe. Most people present will have received the kind of basic teaching given in their denominational confirmation or church membership classes. Unlike preachers, they will not have received the depth of education in Christian doctrine considered essential for ordained and lay preachers. Most church members will receive little other teaching about Christian doctrine, other than what they get in Sunday sermons. Though some will attend Church-run training courses or lectures, these will not be the majority. The only ongoing teaching in the fundamentals of the faith for most Christians will be what they get in church on Sundays.

These facts place great responsibility on all those commissioned to teach the Christian faith.

Teaching doctrine can be boring and some would assert that preaching is not the right medium for it anyway. Nevertheless, Colin Gunton's *Theology Through Preaching* is a good example of how such teaching can be given in a local church.[41] As Professor of Christian Doctrine at King's College, London, Professor Gunton had all the credentials of a first-rate theological teacher. He preached these thirty sermons, however, as Associate Minister of Brentwood United Reformed Church, and demonstrated how preaching about the Creation and the Trinity, the Incarnation and Atonement, and Sin, Grace and Faith can form an integral part of a Sunday morning act of worship. He was careful to point out, however, that such sermons were not first of all to educate his hearers about doctrine, though that was an obvious spin-off from them, but primarily to enable them 'to see the glory of God in the face of Jesus'.

Clearly there are other good ways of teaching doctrine. Church members can attend courses or participate in well-led study groups where they are encouraged to explore what they believe. Because many church members are not involved in such groups, however, much of the responsibility for teaching Christian doctrine returns to preachers. If we fail to do it, it is likely that many church members will continue to miss out.

Preachers are well aware that the Apostles' Creed provides a good outline for a series of sermons about Christian belief. Christian festivals also provide us with ideal opportunities to tackle the fundamentals of faith highlighted then, rather than to avoid them in favour of some of the peripherals. People attending church at

---

[41] Colin Gunton, *Theology Through Preaching*, p.v.

Christmas should expect to hear sermons about the Incarnation, not just about the plight of the homeless and refugees, important though such considerations are. Similarly the message of Easter is not just the resurgence of nature, with chicks bursting out of eggs and daffodils poking their heads through the ground. Rather it is about Christ rising triumphantly over death, a victory which is both a vindication of his claims and an assurance of our future. Then there is Trinity Sunday. A few years ago, a representative of an overseas mission society said his society received more requests for preachers for Trinity Sunday than for any other time. Preachers owe it to their congregations to tackle such subjects, and provided they are able to relate these doctrinal truths to the real life experience and needs of the congregation, they may be surprised at how gladly they are heard.

HOW TO LIVE

Although the Christian life is not just about belief, it is motivated by belief: we become what we are because we believe what we do. Belief and behaviour are inextricably bound together. 'How to live' sermons point to a Christian lifestyle summarised by Christ's command that we should love God and one another, and is spelled out in the New Testament as a whole.

All three of these sub-types of discipleship sermons will contain some biblical content, as is to be expected from Churches claiming that the Bible is normative for both Christian belief and practice. The content of what we have called discipleship sermons, however, and precisely how the Bible is used in them, will be decided by their overriding purpose, which is to build up church members.

STEWARDSHIP SERMONS

Christian Stewardship is a theme running through the life of the Church in all its denominations. Preaching about stewardship, however, should not have to await the arrival of a stewardship adviser for the launching of a stewardship campaign. Although visiting advisers may be helpful, as preachers we need to recognise that stewardship is not something brought into a Christian community from outside but an essential ingredient of what it means to be Christian. All preachers will wish to preach sermons about stewardship, including stewardship of the earth as well as that of possessions and time, gifts and service.

STEWARDSHIP OF THE EARTH

The first of the Bible's creation stories tells us that God created man and woman in his own image and committed to them a stewardship, under him, of the rest of the created order. We may not be supporters of some New-Agers whose care for the earth leads them to adopt various excesses, not least in New Age worship. Nor need we necessarily join those who chain themselves to giant earth movers in a vain attempt to prevent the building of new motorways on the grounds that they will despoil thousands of acres of British countryside and destroy much wildlife. As Christians, however, we surely do believe that God has committed to us the stewardship of the earth, and that we are accountable to him for the way we exercise our stewardship.

The *Faith in the Countryside* report stated so pertinently:

A doctrine of God as creator and lover of the material world implies the necessity of living in that world and being responsible for it in such a way that the attitudes of society as a whole to this relationship with nature will be transformed.[42]

The non-human world of animals, plants and inorganic matter cannot represent its own interests, [the report continued] for this world needs a voice and a champion, now as never before. It is the human race which threatens it, and unless the human being recognises and acts out his role as representative, the free and willing agent of God's purposes, human attitudes will remain at the level of the manipulative or sentimental, and human influences will be demonic.[43]

POSSESSIONS AND TIME

Western society's materialistic self-indulgence should give all preachers sufficient motivation to preach about attitudes to possessions and the money we have to acquire them, as well as time and how we spend it. Is there not a responsible and generous Christian attitude that should override more selfish considerations? Preaching about this is probably much more important than the occasional sermon about Christian giving, when the church treasurer is becoming anxious about a possible shortfall or an unpaid heating bill. Nevertheless, preaching about direct giving to God through the church is also important because, as Paul reminds us, 'God loves a cheerful giver' and giving should be our thankful response to 'his indescribable gift'.[44]

GIFTS AND MINISTRY

In the second half of the twentieth century Christians began to rediscover the two related New Testament truths that God gives 'gifts' to all his people and that all of us are called

---

[42] *Faith in the Countryside,* p.10.
[43] Ibid., p.15.
[44] 2 Corinthians 9:7 and 15.

to use those gifts in 'ministry', that is 'service'. The primary Christian vocation is to discipleship, but within that discipleship God calls and equips church members for different kinds of service. Ministry is not a vocation for a relatively small elite, therefore, but something to which all are called and from which no one is excluded.

Congregations need to be reminded of these truths constantly, not merely because of the decline in the number of full-time, paid, and ordained ministers resulting in gaps having to be filled, but more importantly because the New Testament makes it abundantly clear that a ministry shared by all Christians was the intention from the beginning of the Christian Church. Even today some church members find this idea difficult to take. Preaching about the stewardship of our gifts and service gives preachers, with God's help, an opportunity to recall church members to a New Testament pattern of ministry.

BIOGRAPHICAL SERMONS

Conveniently, these fall into three groups: biblical, historical, and contemporary characters.

BIBLICAL CHARACTERS

Congregations who find listening to the exposition of long Bible passages or Bible themes hard work, will perhaps appreciate a preacher who sometimes approaches the Bible through the biography of one of the Old Testament characters like Moses, David, or Daniel, or the New Testament's Peter, Paul, or John. Nor need preachers always choose major characters, for attention to some of the less prominent figures in the Bible can be very rewarding.

HISTORICAL CHARACTERS

Some of the early Christians, like Polycarp, who was martyred for his loyalty to Christ, make excellent topics, and certainly help congregations to see that the history of the early Church was more exciting, and sometimes more dangerous, than they realised. Sermons about people like Cuthbert, Aidan, Patrick and some of the other early missionaries, will build up an understanding of how Christianity came to Britain. Preaching about Bible translators such as Wycliffe and Tyndale may remind congregations of how easy it is to take for granted the availability of the Bible in a number of English translations, whilst an attempt to link these with the work of a modern translator compiling a written language from scratch would make an interesting comparison. The Reformation period's leading figures on both sides of the Protestant/Catholic divide, and John Bunyan imprisoned in Bedford Gaol, or the Wesleys and William Booth some time later, all provide plentiful resources for some interesting character studies.

CONTEMPORARY CHARACTERS

These have to be treated with care, because they are still alive, but an occasional sermon drawing attention to God's work through one of them has much to offer about Christian fortitude, and may help to prick the bubble that good Christians are always happy, whatever their circumstances.

OUTREACH SERMONS

This sixth type of preaching, which includes evangelistic and apologetic sermons, is particularly important within what is sometimes called a post-Christian Western society. We still claim to be basically Christian in our standards but society at large has lost sight of the faith which teaches and motivates those standards. In their own distinctive ways, evangelistic and apologetic sermons call us back to our Christian roots. Implicitly, and sometimes quite explicitly, they warn of the danger of trying to live off Christian capital.

EVANGELISTIC SERMONS

Evangelism is a much wider ministry than preaching. It includes the witness of Christians in their daily work, in their contact with family and friends, and in their life in the community more generally. Evangelism uses all kinds of agencies and methods, including literature, advertising, films and video recordings, and the internet. In its broadest sense, evangelism is a task for all Christians, not just for those called to a preaching ministry. Nevertheless, all preachers, even those who do not believe they are particularly gifted evangelists, are called to share in the task of evangelism, for they have been called to proclaim the Good News of God's Kingdom. All authentic Christian preaching can claim to be evangelistic, because it is handling some aspect of that Good News.

Some preaching, however, is evangelistic in a much more specific sense. To use words attributed to William Temple and others, its single-minded intention is so to present Christ Jesus in the power of the Holy Spirit, that people may come to put their trust in God through him, to accept him as their Saviour, and serve him as their King in the fellowship of his Church.[45] Evangelistic preaching in this specific sense normally focuses mainly on those aspects of the Gospel which will encourage hearers to move towards personal repentance and faith.

At its best, this kind of preaching has much in common with the *kerygma* (preaching) of the Acts of the Apostles, which in the main took place in the open air. Church history provides many notable examples of direct

---

[45] The 1918 Archbishops' *Committee of Enquiry on the Evangelistic Work of the Church.*

evangelistic preaching, often outside church buildings, including the great eighteenth-century preaching tours of the Wesleys and George Whitefield, and the remarkable nineteenth-century American and British city campaigns of D L Moody which led to many conversions and, with the Wesleys, the founding of the Methodist Church. Similarly, the American evangelist, Dr Billy Graham, conducted hundreds of evangelistic missions during the twentieth century, making use of modern technology to carry his message to many millions of people throughout the world. Such preaching has often been criticised as being over emotional or too narrow in the concept of the Gospel. The fact remains, however, that many thousands of people acknowledge that it was through this kind of evangelistic preaching that they became Christians.

Because of the success of some large-scale evangelistic missions, which have made significant contributions to the growth of the Church, we may be tempted to think that all effective evangelistic preaching has to be of this kind. The Church's continuing evangelistic outreach, however, depends chiefly on the regular ministry of local churches. Hence the need for sermons that clearly present what God offers us in Christ and which encourage people to respond to that offer by their own personal commitment.

Church-based preaching, however, must not be seen as the Church's sole means of evangelism, for the majority of the unconvinced, the uncommitted and the uninterested are not often found in church congregations. Nevertheless some of them do attend church services from time to time, especially for baptisms, weddings, and funerals and on other special occasions like Remembrance Sunday, Harvest, Christmas and Easter. As long as the preaching is done appropriately and with sensitivity, such occasions provide an opportunity for the clear and challenging presentation of the Good News. Nor should we assume that regular churchgoers do not need to be faced with clear evangelistic challenges from time to time.

APOLOGETIC SERMONS

Alongside sermons which are directly evangelistic, there is also a place for apologetic preaching which puts forward a reasoned defence of, and argument for, the claims of Christianity. Topics like *Can we prove that God exists?*, *If there is a God, why does he allow evil and suffering?*, *What historical evidence is there for Jesus Christ?*, and *Can a scientist be a Christian?* are well worth airing from time to time. Provided such sermons do not turn into heavy, over-academic lectures, they can help to encourage churchgoers to apply their thinking to their faith and to deal with the kind of arguments levelled against Christianity which they often meet in their daily life. Alister McGrath has shown that apologetic sermons can also help the unconvinced to see that Christianity is not blind, unthinking belief.[46] All of this is in keeping with the New Testament exhortation 'to contend for the faith which was once for all delivered to the saints'.[47]

HISTORICAL SERMONS

This last of the sermon types gives preachers the opportunity to show to their congregations the broad historical context in which they can understand how and why the Church has developed in the way it has. As we have seen already, some of this kind of preaching can be covered in biographical sermons, but there is also room for a broad-brush approach that explains how Christianity came to Britain, or how the different denominations came into being. At a different level, the occasional sermon about the

---

[46] McGrath, *Bridge Building*, p.9.
[47] Jude 3.

development of Christianity in the immediate locality of the congregation's own church, can be interesting and helpful, particularly if it can be tied in with past members who played a significant part in that development.

TYPES AND STEREOTYPES

Trying to confine any sermon to a single type is often difficult and sometimes impossible. A sermon may be classed as biblical because it explains a Bible passage, but at the same time be regarded as topical because it also addresses a contemporary issue and seeks to apply the teaching of the Bible passage to it. Another sermon may be classed as a 'what to believe' sermon because it outlines Christian belief about the Cross, but can also be called evangelistic because it urges people to respond to what God has done for them in Christ. There are no hard and fast rules.

How valuable is it, then, for preachers to concern themselves with sermon types? At the very least it serves as a necessary reminder to use a variety of sermon types rather than to allow their preaching to follow a single stereotype. Originally, a stereotype was a solid metallic plate used in printing. Before the advent of computer software removed many of the old traditional printing skills, a craftsman would work hard at the plate to produce by hand the image required. The original plate then became the stereotype which would be used to produce many other identical images.

Nowadays, we are more likely to use 'stereotype' to describe the behaviour, work, or activity of a person who always seems to conform to a particular image. Caricatures of the trendy vicars provide timely reminders that clergy are not immune from the danger of allowing themselves slavishly to follow trends, and this certainly includes preachers. Later we shall see how important it is for preachers to be themselves as they preach. Here we simply note that neither preachers nor their sermons have to conform to any stereotypes. Awareness of the wide range of sermon types may encourage preachers to avoid this pitfall.

4. PRELIMINARIES

The following incident helps to highlight some of the pitfalls that may befall preachers and the essential groundwork needed to try to avoid them.

On a cold winter's day, eight faithful communicants assembled in a large church for an 8 a.m. Holy Communion service. Their average age was seventy. The president was younger than all but one of his congregation, the exception being a young man who had dropped into the service on his way to work.

Because the president believed firmly that Word and Sacrament belonged together and always preached at a Communion service, he read the set epistle, 1 Corinthians 7:1–11, and then proceeded to expound the passage in some detail. He spoke forcefully, and at some length, about human sexuality, challenging his small and rather cold congregation to apply their Christianity to their personal sexual behaviour. Then he completed the communion service and went home for breakfast, no doubt thinking that he had faithfully fulfilled his responsibility as a minister of Word and Sacrament.

In contrast, his congregation were left feeling that the sermon had been unnecessary, largely irrelevant to their needs, but above all quite inappropriate on this occasion.

There were two good things about this sermon. First, the preacher, following what some would regard as a golden rule for preachers, used one of the set Bible readings for his sermon. Secondly, he attempted to relate the Bible's teaching to life today. You may think, however, that he chose the wrong time and the wrong congregation for this particular sermon.

We should not be too hard in our criticism, for most

preachers have made similar mistakes. Would you have preached this kind of sermon in those circumstances? How might the sermon have been different if the preacher had taken more account of the occasion, the temperature, and the size and average age of the congregation? Nevertheless, this incident demonstrates clearly that there are some important preliminary questions all preachers need to ask before the work of preparing to preach can begin in earnest. They concern the *time*, the *place*, the *congregation* and the *service*.

TIME

At what time will the sermon be preached? This obvious question needs to be asked, not simply because as preachers we need to be at the church on time, but also because it has a number of related implications for the kind of sermon that can be preached on that occasion. Consider, for example, the time implications of three different services: an 8 a.m. service in the depths of winter, a midnight communion service on Christmas Eve, and a mid-morning service on a summer's day.

For the early morning winter communion service the church may be cold and the congregation small. Some will not have been out of bed for more than thirty minutes. Most will expect to be home for breakfast by 9 a.m. at the latest.

At the other extreme, the Christmas midnight service will probably have a larger congregation than usual. Some may be visitors, others local residents putting in their annual appearance, a few will be in high spirits having come on from a Christmas Eve party, others may feel tired and jaded because it is late and they have been working hard in the build-up to Christmas, and a handful may be dreading the next few days because of bereavement and loneliness.

Some of the mid-morning summer congregation may intend to go on to other activities as soon as the service ends, and there will be those who have left their Sunday joints cooking. Many will be keeping an anxious eye on their watches if the preacher seems to be taking too much time, or if the service as a whole appears to be dragging.

As preachers we may not like to be reminded of such mundane matters, pretending that our congregations have their thoughts on much holier matters. Unless we are realistic, however, our preaching may be counterproductive. The length and theme of a sermon which may be appropriate in the more leisurely context of a normal Sunday service will not always be appreciated at other times. I recall one very distinguished preacher holding forth for twenty-five minutes at a midnight Christmas communion service. He was not very popular!

PLACE

Where will the sermon be preached? Apart from the obvious need to be in the right place at the right time, there are other less obvious implications for the kind of sermon that can be preached in a particular place. We need to be very clear about them. Is the building a well-attended city centre church, or one in a sparsely populated and remote village? Is it large or small, old or modern, cold or warm, comfortable or uncomfortable? What are the implications if the service, or part of it, is to take place outside the church at the local War Memorial on Remembrance Sunday, or in a community hall or school on a new housing development? Questions about location ought to figure prominently at the beginning of preparation.

Some church buildings lend themselves to a formal, and others to a less formal, way of preaching. What may be appreciated in one, may not be welcomed in another. We need to be aware of, and sensitive to, people's feelings about their church buildings and take special care not to ride roughshod over any local sensitivities.

A cold building with uncomfortable pews is unlikely to encourage people to listen to a long sermon, no matter how eloquent the preacher may be. A building designed to seat the congregation in the round and not too distant from the preacher may be conducive to a more intimate kind of preaching, but a large building with a scattered congregation is bound to lack that kind of intimacy. Perhaps the worst scenario is a modern building with antique furnishings handed down from a redundant church. Whatever the local situation, we can begin to prepare appropriately only if we know what we shall be facing when we arrive to preach.

As preachers we need to discover all we can about the building's acoustics. If there is an amplification system, is it effective or ineffective? Is it possible to try it out before the service begins, preferably before the congregation arrives? Most systems require disciplined users, only the best being able to cope with over-mobile preachers. If there is no amplification system and the church is large, it will help to spend a few minutes with a helper, trying to ensure that we can be heard.

Eye contact helps speakers to hold people's attention and to gauge how well they are receiving what is being said. Not every church building enables preacher and congregation to see each other; and no matter how hard preachers try, some members of congregations will always defeat them by hiding behind thick pillars. We must be prepared for any difficulties a building may present. The unhelpful habit of trying to save money by turning off some of the lights during sermons is something that every preacher should try to discourage, though visiting preachers have to handle such situations with sensitivity.

Good visibility is especially important if preachers are

planning to use visual aids. Not every church building is suitable for their use and not every preacher is good at producing them. To state the obvious, congregations do not take kindly to the use of inferior or *invisible* aids. If there is any doubt about the suitability of the building or the quality of the material, it is better not to use visual aids on that occasion and in that place. The overhead projector with the sun shining directly onto its screen, and the flip chart with words too small to be read by all, are to be avoided at all costs.

CONGREGATION

We also need to know as much as possible about the congregation to whom we are preparing to preach. 'Researching the audience is probably the most neglected aspect of speech preparation,' writes Anne Nicholls.[48] Preachers need to heed that warning just as much as the more general public speakers to whom those words were written.

No form of communication happens in a vacuum and uniquely preaching owes its effectiveness to the fact that it is shaped by God's revelation of himself embodied in Christ, available through scripture, and coming alive through God's Spirit. We must never forget, however, that it also depends on the nature of the encounter between preacher and congregation. Whenever possible, we must prepare sermons that are tailor-made to particular congregations. Unless we speak to people's real needs, we should not complain if our message is ignored.

When congregations consist largely of regular churchgoers, those preaching on home ground may feel they know something of the congregation's background and

---

[48] Anne Nicholls, *How to Master Public Speaking*, p.22.

tradition, as well as the assumptions that it may be safe to make about their knowledge and commitment. When preaching in other places, however, we need to be briefed. It is equally important to know when those who are not regular churchgoers are expected on special occasions. Regular churchgoers may need, and can usually take, a different kind of sermon from a mixed congregation with a number who do not normally attend. All preachers need to think carefully about the kind of preaching appropriate for their specific congregations.

Information about the age range of congregations is also important. It can all go embarrassingly wrong when preachers do not obtain or receive such basic information. I attended a service where the preacher had been led to expect that a large proportion of the congregation would be children. Accordingly, she prepared a sermon with a number of simple visual aids and was expecting some enthusiastic participation from her congregation. On the day, three children turned up and the rest of the congregation were not prepared to enter into the spirit of the occasion! In contrast, it often happens that no allowances are made for children in a congregation. They are expected to sit through a sermon, which is far above their heads. As preachers we cannot always get it right, but there is no excuse for not trying!

The size of the congregation, as well as its age range and the parts of the community it represents, always needs to be taken into account. Congregations large and small have an equal right to expect their preachers to proclaim some aspect of the Good News of God's Kingdom. The validity of the message does not depend upon the number of people present. Nevertheless, we should not ignore the expected size of the congregation, for that will help us to decide what, how, and perhaps how long, to preach.

It is also worth mentioning that short sermons are not

necessarily easier to prepare than long ones. One of my friends has been known to append to his longer letters a note reading, 'I'm sorry this letter is so long, but I hadn't time to write a short one.'

SERVICE

The precise context of the preaching is another important factor for preachers to consider. The possibilities range widely: a liturgical pattern following a denominational service book; an informal family service; a service of Holy Communion or baptism; or a service for a special time of the year like Christmas, Easter or Harvest. What is appropriate in one context may be inappropriate in another.

The answers to all of these preliminary questions are the essential groundwork for all preachers and will help them to decide the kind of preaching appropriate at a particular time, in a specific place, on that occasion, and within the context of a specific form of service. Such planning can save preachers and hearers much anxiety, heartache, frustration and disappointment. Maybe the sermon of that well-meaning preacher with whom we began this chapter would have been better received if he had taken the trouble to do this preliminary groundwork.

Members of the congregation need to be educated about the importance of the sermon within the act of worship. Their role in helping to make the preaching effective should include prayer for the preacher and for themselves as listeners. They need to be encouraged to believe that God may be speaking through the preacher to them individually and corporately, and hopefully to respond. Occasionally you may wish to tell your congregation that a remark like 'Lovely sermon, vicar!' may be less helpful than a positive comment or question, and subsequent discussion, arising from what has been said.

Ezekiel warns us that there are right and wrong ways of listening to those proclaiming God's message. At the time when Jews were exiled in Babylonia, the prophet was told,

> As for you, mortal, your people who talk together about you by the walls, and at the doors of the houses, say to one another, each to a neighbour, 'Come and hear what the word is that comes from the Lord.' They come to you as people come, and they sit before you as my people, and they hear your words, but they will not obey them … To them you are like a singer of love songs, one who has a beautiful voice, and plays well on an instrument; they hear what you say, but they will not do it.[49]

Hearers as well as preachers have work to do if preaching is to be effective.

---

[49] Ezekiel 33:30ff.

CHECKLIST ONE – PRELIMINARIES

WHAT MIGHT INFLUENCE YOUR PREPARATION?

At what time of the day will you will be preaching?

- Early morning;
- Middle of the day;
- Early evening;
- Late at night.

Where will you be preaching?

- A large church in a town centre;
- A small church in a sparsely populated village;
- A large church with limited facilities;
- A modern church with up-to-date facilities;
- Somewhere completely different.

To what kind of congregation will you be preaching?

- An ageing congregation;
- A mixture of old, middle-aged, and young, with some parents and their children;
- College lecturers and their students;
- A parade service for local youth organisations.

During which type of service will you be preaching?

- A service with a liturgical pattern using a denominational service book;
- An informal service with a music group;
- A family service which encourages all-age learning through a question and answer approach;
- A service marking a special occasion.

5. THEMES

Previous chapters have attempted to give an overview of preaching. We must turn now to what might be called the 'nuts and bolts' of sermon preparation, concerning ourselves with the specific steps any preacher has to take to prepare a particular sermon for a specific occasion in a particular place. I am assuming that all of us who prepare to preach recognise, with the apostles in Acts 6:4, that our ministry is one of 'prayer' as well as of 'the ministry of the Word', and that we all realise our need to rely on God to guide us through every stage of our preparation. As is often said, however, we should not pray for something unless we are willing to work hard to bring it about. Here as always our prayer needs to be translated into action.

How might we take the first steps in preparation? As good a way as any is to work through those essential preliminaries outlined in Chapter 2. The checklist on page 71 suggests the way. The first step in sermon preparation is to decide on a sermon theme. Later it will be necessary to produce a more specific aim, but this part of the preparation is concerned only with the theme or topic, the general area that the sermon will try to cover. Someone inviting you to preach may suggest a theme, especially if your sermon is to be one of a series. More usually you will be left to choose your own.

Related questions about how many there are likely to be in church when we preach, whether or not they will be regular churchgoers and/or visitors unused to church services, and the age range they represent, are all essential pieces of information that will help to determine the choice of a theme. Bearing in mind that a sermon is not preached in a vacuum, we must also take into account the form and content of the service as we consider our theme. Hopefully we shall choose the hymns or will be consulted about them. We shall want to do all we can to ensure that hymns, prayers, and everything about the service will contribute to the theme, at the same time being careful to see the sermon, not as an end in itself, but as an important element in the whole act of worship on that occasion.

THEMES AND THE BIBLE

No preacher should need to be reminded of the great privilege and tremendous responsibility of what we are preparing to do. Preaching is 'a manifestation of the Incarnate Word, from the written Word, by the spoken word'.[50] The preaching roles outlined in Chapter 3 underline this responsibility and privilege and will help to motivate us as our preparation proceeds. Everyone who preaches has a sense of inadequacy and may wish to echo Paul's words: 'There is nothing in us that allows us to claim that we are capable of doing this work. The capacity we have comes from God.'[51]

Working with the Bible as our chief resource and focusing on the set Bible readings, we may find it helpful to ask ourselves four questions:

- What are the themes of the passages? It goes without saying that we do not have to deal with them all, but more about that later.
- Does anything stand out in these readings as an appropriate theme for our sermon on this occasion?
- What might God first be saying through it to me? As

[50] Sangster, *The Craft of Sermon Construction*, p.4.
[51] 2 Corinthians 3:5 (GNB).

noted elsewhere, preachers have first to *preach to themselves*; for unless the Bible passage comes alive to us as we prepare, we are unlikely to be able to make it come alive to those who hear us.

- What might God wish to say through us to the congregation?

OTHER RESOURCES

Taking it for granted that the Bible is our main resource in preparing to preach, the following diagram illustrates the sources of additional material which can be used to help with a chosen theme.

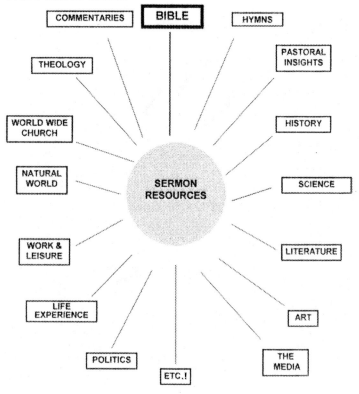

All resources have their part to play, sometimes contributing to a sermon's substance, at other times providing illustrations that help to make it come alive, but first among them are those which help to throw light on the meaning of your Bible passage and its contemporary application.

Bible commentaries are an indispensable resource in this process and will help preachers to avoid some of the more obvious errors. Although we should not be the first preachers to build a sermon on the shaky foundation of a misunderstanding of the text, a good commentary may help to avoid such pitfalls. Moreover, because one of the preaching roles is to teach, anything that can be done to help dispel the growing ignorance of the Bible, even among people in the pews, will be invaluable. Again, when we take the trouble to read what others have written about the Bible, our own thought processes will be stimulated and ideas will begin to appear.

After such careful study, we shall be ready to consider other resource materials to supplement all gained from Bible study. In this respect we can learn from birds of the crow family who have a highly developed hoarding instinct. Jackdaws and magpies are particularly notorious for their habit of collecting shiny or coloured objects and anything else that takes their fancy, as well as food. Nests have been found full of such objects, hoarded away for some future purpose. Many preachers have developed a similar 'jackdaw instinct' by collecting suitable sermon resource materials. Some keep a preacher's notebook into which they are constantly making notes for possible use in future sermons. They are following a well-trodden path, for through the years many preachers, speakers, and other public performers have done the same.

Richard Briers, for over thirty years one of the most versatile British stage and television performers, is a good contemporary example. Describing how he sharpened up his conversation skills, he writes,

I tried to make a point of noting down something every day. Bon mots, pithy aphorisms, amusing anecdotes, jargon, or simply neat ways of expressing the commonplace, all found their way into my little book. The process certainly reaped its rewards. My memory started to improve and I became far more attentive to what was going on around me.[52]

Whether or not we follow that practice precisely, collecting a ready store of resources that can be used as the need arises, we shall certainly need to begin assembling resource materials for sermons as soon as we can, and not less than a week before we are to preach.

Having lived opposite a large new housing development for some years, I know that building sites are not noted for their tidiness. Long before any pattern emerges, lorries arrive with monotonous regularity, and all too often at the break of day, to offload building materials for future use. At first the casual onlooker might wonder if it will ever be possible to turn this untidy mass into the smart new houses that have been promised. As time passes, however, a clear pattern begins to emerge, a well-designed housing development arises from the apparent chaos, and eventually newcomers move in to benefit from all the construction efforts that have gone before.

This building site analogy may help as we begin the task of assembling the resource materials out of which our sermon will be constructed. One well-tried way of proceeding is to write on a large sheet of paper anything that comes to mind about the chosen theme. Random jottings might include: study notes of the Bible passage from which the theme has been derived; thoughts and ideas, memories and experiences, study of the Bible passage may have helped us to dig out; and contributions to the theme gathered from

---

[52] Richard Briers, *Natter, Natter*, p.41.

that great wealth of resource materials available alongside that of the Bible.

Eventually we need to decide on a short, specific aim to help us to become more selective in our use of the resource material, but that comes later. The task at this stage is to work creatively, so it is helpful to write down anything that may have the slightest bearing on the proposed general theme. An experienced trainer of public speakers suggests how the process works. 'The brain does not work in a "logical" pattern: if you start by writing an outline then you are imposing order before you have had a chance to generate ideas.'[53] This well-tried method works for preachers and other public speakers alike, and it – or something like it – is worth adopting.

The wealth of collected resource materials then begin to prove their worth. If, for example, a sermon is intended to raise people's concern about world hunger or poverty, magazines published by Christian Aid, Tearfund, Oxfam, and similar organisations provide a mine of information. For a sermon about life after death, it may be helpful to put alongside the illustrations used by Paul in 1 Corinthians 15, information gleaned from natural history books of how caterpillars are transformed into butterflies. Whatever the topic, an initial uninhibited brainstorming session should result in a sheet of paper covered with suggestions which provide the raw material out of which we shall be able to build a sermon.

Disciplined and discriminating use of hymns can add something to our own words and strike chords with some people, and may help to crystallise our own thinking and so form a useful part of preparation.

As was suggested earlier, proper planning of the complete service, including the choice of hymns which

---

[53] Anne Nicholls, *How to Master Public Speaking,* p.42.

relate to the sermon's theme, will help the congregation to see a single theme running through the whole act of worship. The careful choice of the hymn to be sung immediately after the sermon is especially important, for its words can help either to reinforce what the preacher has said or provide the congregation with a way of responding to what they have heard.

One of the assumptions of this book is that we face up to our responsibility as preachers by keeping our theology up to date through regular reading. Alongside this, some sermons require extra reading as we prepare. For example, we may need to give particular attention to theology and Church teaching if our sermon is to touch on cardinal Christian doctrines or important pastoral and ethical issues. Many minds greater than ours have wrestled for centuries with such matters as the doctrine of the Trinity, and the Person and Work of Christ. We shall also be aware of the teaching contained in the historic Christian creeds and the doctrinal formularies of the Christian Church. Although sermons should never be turned into lectures with heavy and undigested doctrine, congregations will appreciate well-prepared attempts to grapple with some of the great truths Christians often take for granted.

Even the most experienced preachers, however, need to read or reread some doctrine before preaching such sermons. One of our tasks is to teach the faith: and, although we shall wish to encourage the faithful to think, we shall need to tread carefully when dealing with controversial and sensitive issues which may disturb some hearers. We must aim always to avoid an arrogant disregard of people's sensitivities, though inevitably, if we are true to what we proclaim, some people will take issue with what we say. Perhaps one of the biggest dangers facing preachers, however, is that of preaching heresy out of ignorance. Attention to theological reading should help us to avoid this.

Every branch of the Christian Church has its boards, councils and committees which produce good educational material on marriage and divorce, sexuality, euthanasia, and a wide range of other contemporary ethical and pastoral issues. From time to time, such matters will need to be aired in the pulpit, but when we decide to tackle them we need first to make ourselves aware of what our church says about them. There is room for difference of viewpoint among Christians, and most congregations will recognise this, but as preachers we have no excuse for that lack of preparation which can so easily lead to the careless dissemination of ignorance.

The pastoral insights gained from daily contact with our families, friends and congregations, as well as with people at work and in the community, may also help to prepare sermons that are both interesting and relevant. To benefit from them, however, we need to be at least as good at listening as we aspire to be at speaking. Such careful listening, whether in everyday informal conversations or arranged pastoral encounters, will help us to become more aware of people's needs and concerns and provide some of the information gathering that is essential in our sermon preparation.

We must take care, however, not to break any confidences shared with us. In a tightly knit community, for example, it is all too easy for members of the congregation to identify the person involved in a situation the preacher uses to make a sermon point. Long-suffering members of preachers' families need special protection from well-meaning parents who all too readily use stories about their children as sermon illustrations. Although references to real life situations can help to make preaching come alive, they need to be used sensitively and sparingly. Moreover, they need to be disguised and described in general terms to avoid personal embarrassment or offence. If we depart from such standards of good practice, we may find that our sermons are counterproductive and our pastoral opportunities diminished. People will be reluctant to talk to us about their pastoral needs if they fear their 'problem' may be drawn to people's attention in next Sunday's sermon.

The resources mentioned so far are mostly of a religious nature, but we also need to remember the great wealth of other resources surrounding us in our daily life. It includes nature, science and technology; work, sport and leisure; politics; literature, especially biography and autobiography; church and secular history; the Church overseas; television and national and local radio; Church newspapers; art, including examples found in church buildings; and our own life experience. The possibilities are endless. Ordained preachers, who have a natural tendency to focus on 'religious' resources, need to balance that by employing some of these 'non-religious' resources in their preparation. This will help to safeguard them from becoming too inward looking, and protect their congregations from over-churchy sermons. On the other hand, lay preachers should not be reluctant to make full use of their out-of-church experience, for this may well be where their particular contribution in preaching lies. At the same time, they should complement all that they have to offer as lay people with those 'religious' resources that most clergy take for granted.

CHECKLIST TWO – THEMES

After studying the Bible readings chosen for the day:

- Consider what are their main themes.
- Focus on one appropriate theme for your sermon.
- What is that theme saying to you?
- What might it say through you to the congregation?

Before making a final decision about your theme, think carefully about whether it is suitable:

- For that time;
- In that place;
- For that congregation;
- In that service;
- For you to handle.

CHECKLIST THREE – RESOURCES

Write your theme at the top of a large sheet of paper and then:

- Make notes of all information gathered about the theme in your study of the Bible passage from which it is derived, particularly notes made in your use of Bible commentaries.
- Allow time to do some creative thinking (brainstorming), jotting down thoughts, ideas, illustrations, anything that appears to be in any way relevant to your theme.
- Try to avoid imposing any orderly arrangement on the collected resources at this stage, remembering that the marshalling of your material will come later when you have clarified your aim.

6. AIMS

To produce an aim which is specific, appropriate and achievable, and to state it as simply, clearly and briefly as possible, is one of the hardest parts of sermon preparation, and can be very time consuming. Equally, to create a sermon structure or framework capable of carrying out that aim is just as important and can be just as difficult. Neither can be skimped. Each must be given enough time if it is to be achieved. An effective sermon needs both. In this chapter we deal with a sermon's aim and in Chapter 7 with sermon structure.

'Aim at nothing and you will hit it every time' is an axiom especially appropriate for preachers. We must be clear about the sermon's aim, or what some writers call its purpose or intention. Clarifying aims is one of the most neglected stages of sermon preparation. Every sermon needs an aim and that aim must be specific, appropriate, achievable, and simple.

A SPECIFIC AIM

Dr Edward Goulburn, a nineteenth-century Dean of Norwich, wrote in his diary on Sunday, 30 December 1883, 'At eleven, the Bishop preached on the General Judgement, quoting almost every text on the subject.'[54] To give him his due, Dr John Pelham, the respected bishop to whom Goulburn referred, was normally a good preacher. Perhaps on this occasion it was a temporary lapse, for we are left wondering with his dean whether he had thought carefully

---

[54] Noel Henderson, *The Goulburn Norwich Diaries*, p.329.

enough about his aim.

At the time of the Second World War, another bishop was asked to speak to a convention on the impossibly wide-ranging theme of 'The World, the War, and the Church'. He responded rather sharply, 'I should like to address your convention. However, I should not like to be cramped in my style or restricted in my remarks by such a narrow subject. I shall be glad to come if you will add to it "the Sun, the Moon, and the Stars".'[55]

You have probably heard preachers who try to cover in a single sermon everything there is to say about a topic. A few years ago I listened to a sermon about prayer which lasted more than forty minutes and which contained the following related but different aspects of the topic:

- Prayer in the Old and New Testaments;
- Jesus at prayer;
- What we think we are doing when we pray;
- What to pray about;
- When and how to pray;
- Why some prayers are not answered in the way we expect;
- Etc., etc., etc.!

This sermon contained much that was worthy of more thought than the congregation was able to give it on that occasion, but the fault was the preacher's, not theirs. He had made a fundamental preaching error. Having chosen 'prayer' as his general theme, he had failed to decide on a specific aim for his sermon. The result was clear to everybody except the preacher, who remained completely insensitive to how his sermon was being received. Although

[55] 2 Prochnow, op. cit., p.78.

it was packed with good material, it was diffuse, involved, lengthy and somewhat tedious, leaving the congregation bewildered, battered, and suffering from spiritual indigestion. Every aspect of prayer covered by this sincere preacher was important. What he failed to realise was that each aspect was so important that it warranted a separate sermon. This is a common enough preaching error which can easily be avoided if preachers discipline themselves to produce an aim which is specific rather than general.

THEMES AND AIMS

At this point we need to be clear about the difference between a general theme and a specific aim. As seen in Chapter 5, a theme is fairly wide ranging, indicating the general topic of the sermon, for example *commitment*, *discipleship,* or *witness*. An aim is much narrower, focusing much more sharply on one specific aspect of the wider general theme.

The difference between the two is illustrated by the sermon about prayer just considered. The preacher's general theme was obviously prayer. But what was his specific aim? It could have been any one of six or more aspects of prayer; but because the preacher tried to deal fully with everything, he failed to deal adequately with anything.

We can all learn from John Henry Newman: 'As a marksman aims at his target and its bull's-eye, and at nothing else, so the preacher must have a definite point before him, which he has to hit.'[56] The general theme of a sermon will usually suggest itself without any difficulty, but the specific aim is something which most preachers need to work hard to achieve.

---

[56] John Henry Newman, *The Idea of a University*, 1852, Part II, Chapter VI.

CONSIDER SOME EXAMPLES

The Bible reading might be Mark 10:13–16, the story of Jesus blessing the young children brought by their parents and his rebuke to the disciples for trying to discourage them. Having chosen Baptism as the theme, and having spent some time studying the passage with the aid of one or more good commentaries, the preacher may begin to jot down on a large sheet of paper everything that springs to mind from his Bible study, wider reading, and other resources – anything at all which seems to have some bearing on the general Baptism theme.

Then the preacher takes another look at all the assembled resource material, the 'building site', and quickly reaches the conclusion that there is no way that all that has been collected can be used in a single sermon. Realising that the focus needs to be much sharper, the preacher asks perhaps the most important question that preachers can ask when preparing sermons: *What specifically do I want to achieve in this sermon on this occasion, bearing in mind this particular congregation?* Depending on the answer, the preacher might then decide to focus specifically on any one, but only one, of the following aims, or indeed on something just as specific but quite different:

- To show that in baptism the initiative is with God, not us.
- To help church members consider whether it is ever right to refuse baptism.
- To indicate ways in which the congregation can help parents and their baptised children.
- To examine the biblical evidence for infant baptism.
- To encourage parents to help their children to fulfil their baptism vows.

Although all five would have baptism as their theme, the specific aim of each would be quite distinct and would result in five different sermons.

On another occasion, the reading might be Hebrews 11 and the general theme Faith. After following the usual preliminary preparatory work, a preacher may decide on any one of the following specific aims, each focusing on a different aspect of faith:

- To show that Christian faith means trust, not just belief.
- To show that faith is about taking risks.
- To help people see that real faith leads to action.
- To consider what faith costs.

All four sermons will be on the same theme, but each will be different because the preacher has prepared it with a specific aim, purpose or intention in mind. With Newman there is a definite target which the preacher is aiming to hit.

AN APPROPRIATE AIM

Another standard question to ask is whether the aim is *appropriate for this occasion and with this congregation?* Once more Newman helps. 'The preacher aims at the divine glory, not in any vague and general way, but definitely by the enunciation of some article or principle of the revealed Word.' So, further, he states, 'It is not for the instruction of the whole world, but for the sake of the very persons before him.' Newman adds, 'We cannot determine how in detail we ought to preach until we know whom we are to address.'[57]

Let us put ourselves in the position of a preacher using the baptism theme considered earlier. Each of the suggested aims

---

[57] Ibid.

is specific, focusing sharply on just one aspect of the general theme, but is each aim also appropriate? To answer that question, we need to consider who will be in the congregation and what their needs and expectations might be.

Will the congregation include young and old members of a family, some of whom do not normally attend church, but all of whom are united in bringing the baby to be baptised? If that is the case, the preacher is unlikely to want to embark on a deep doctrinal discussion of the pros and cons of infant baptism. Instead, an aim designed to encourage parents to bring up children in a Christian environment might seem much more appropriate.

Supposing, however, the sermon follows lengthy, controversial in-church discussions about the church's baptism policy. Opinions have been sharply divided about whether the children of all-comers should be baptised irrespective of any evidence of Christian commitment; or whether parents and godparents should be expected to demonstrate their Christian commitment in some way. For example, should they be required to attend preparation sessions and church services? A thoughtful, balanced and sensitive sermon asking whether it is ever right to refuse baptism may be just what is needed – though it is hardly the first one an inexperienced preacher would wish to preach! In that case the question about appropriateness has to be widened to include not only the appropriateness of the sermon's aim on that occasion and for that congregation, but also if that preacher is an appropriate person to preach it.

AN ACHIEVABLE AIM

Like Christian disciples generally, preachers should have high ideals. Their concerns should include the spread of the Gospel worldwide, the building up of the Christian Church, the transformation of society, and the coming of

God's Kingdom. Good though such high ideals are, they do not provide preachers with achievable aims for sermons, although from time to time preachers will hope and pray that their sermons will make a small contribution towards them. We have to be realistic, however, about what might be an achievable aim within the ten, fifteen, or twenty minutes allotted to the sermon? A realistic aim can do no more than to proclaim an *aspect* of the Good News, to show our congregation a *facet* of God's truth, to present a *particular challenge* to God's people.

Look back to the Baptism theme based on Mark 10 and the faith theme based on Hebrews 11. The suggested aims for each of these are not perfect but may be considered achievable. The third of those arising from Hebrews 11, 'to help people see that real faith leads to action', specifies the particular aspect of faith on which it is planned to focus on one occasion. As the sermon develops we have an achievable aim, for it is possible to show that in all the examples cited by the writer faith led to action. That in turn could become a challenge to the congregation. What about our faith? Is it mere belief, or does it lead us to act? The other aims mentioned for sermons on baptism and faith would lead to different sermons on other occasions. The starting point for any of them is the succinct statement of a specific, appropriate and achievable aim.

A SIMPLE AIM

Here we must distinguish between the sermon's aim and its content. No matter how profound the sermon might turn out to be, the preacher should always be able to state its aim in a single, simple sentence. Think again of the meandering sermon on prayer described earlier. It is extremely doubtful whether, in preparing that sermon, the preacher got further than thinking about the general theme, prayer. With the benefit of hindsight, we may hazard a guess of his reply had he been asked afterwards to state his aim. It might have been something like this:

> To give the congregation a brief résumé of the teaching about prayer in the Old and New Testaments; to ask them to consider more specifically Jesus at prayer; to get them to ask what they think they are doing when they pray; to encourage them to think carefully what they should pray about and when and how they should pray; and to suggest why some prayers are not answered in the way expected.

That aim is expressed in a long involved sentence of seventy-three words with five clauses, any one of which would have provided an aim for a sermon. As it is, there is no specific and achievable aim, and whatever aim the preacher may have had in mind cannot be expressed in a simple, brief sentence. As a result, the sermon seems to wander hither and thither, with the preacher never sure about which aspect of the very laudable but general theme of prayer he is trying to develop.

The lesson for all preachers is obvious. If our aim requires an involved sentence containing several clauses and many words, we have got it wrong and must try again. The renowned preacher, J H Jowett, said that no sermon was ready to preach until the preacher could express its aim in a 'short, pregnant sentence as clear as a crystal'. He added that, although he found that to be the hardest and most exacting part of his preparation, he was sure that no sermon should be preached until that sentence had emerged 'clear and lucid as a cloudless moon'.[58]

---

[58] G H Dovan, *Jowett, the Preacher: his life and work*, p.133.

CHECKLIST FOUR – AIMS

Make a careful review of:

- your general theme;
- the resources you have gathered which are relevant to it;
- decide which one of the many aspects of the theme you wish to deal with.

Work on one aspect of the theme to produce a single aim that is:

- specific, rather than general;
- appropriate for the particular congregation to which it will be preached and for you to preach it;
- realistic enough for you to hope to achieve it;
- capable of being expressed in a single short, simple sentence.

Revise aim as necessary, bearing in mind the guidelines above.

Throughout the rest of your preparation, return to your one specific aim to ensure that you have not wandered from it.

7. STRUCTURES

'There are two classes of sermon; the vertebrate and the invertebrate,' a nineteenth-century bishop told preachers. He urged them to 'make the backbone and the skeleton strong'.[59] He was talking sense, for without the strength of a reliable structure, a sermon is likely to be disjointed, unmanageable, and disorganised. Every preacher needs a dependable framework within which to develop the sermon's pattern, shape, movement and direction and to give it coherence. A strong and reliable structure is as vital to a sermon as a skeleton is to a body.

When we have chosen our theme, assembled our materials, and clarified our aim, therefore, the next task is to deal with the proposed sermon's structure. We need what has been called a basic, stripped-down, unfleshed structural design.[60] This will give the strength of a good skeleton, the plan of a well-designed building, and the direction of an orderly layout.

Such a sermon structure will need unity, order, balance and direction. The needed unity will be that of a single purpose arising from the aim. The order within the structure will enable the sermon to contain logical development from beginning to end. The structure's balance will help to ensure that each section of the sermon is given as much emphasis as its importance warrants. The structure's direction will move the sermon on through each section to its planned conclusion.

Time and effort designing well thought out structures will

---

[59] Cited in Gordon Ireson, *How Shall They Hear?,* p.63.
[60] Buttrick, op. cit., p.308.

be well spent and benefit preachers and congregations alike. We shall be able to build around our structures sermons that will achieve our aims. Our congregations will feel confident that we know where we are going. It was said of one famous preacher, F W Robertson, that, whenever he preached, he made it easy for the hearer to see the skeleton of his sermons.[61] We may not always wish to make our structure quite so obvious, but none of our hearers should be left in any doubt that there is a strong and dependable structure underlying what is being preached.

STAGES IN STRUCTURAL DESIGN

Something like the following procedure will lead from aim, through resources, to structure. First we need to remind ourselves of what specifically we are aiming to achieve in our sermon. That is crucial, for aim and structure belong together and depend on each other. If the proposed structure does not help us to achieve our aim, then it must be discarded or changed. Secondly, we shall need to review our resources. Working through notes made in our earlier preparation, we shall be able to consider which parts of that collected biblical and other material will help us to achieve our aim, for that will also have a bearing on the kind of framework our sermon needs. Then, in the light of these two steps, we shall be ready to begin planning the sermon structure itself. As we try out some first drafts, we shall begin to favour one rather than the others as the most suitable for our purpose. The checklist at the end of this chapter outlines the process.

As suggested earlier, it may be necessary to try several draft structures before we can arrive at one which works best for the sermon and which we feel happy to use. We can then settle for that and discard the others.

---

[61] Andrew Blackwood, *The Preparation of Sermons*, p.138.

STRUCTURAL SKILLS

Sangster said that sermons belonged to one of five structural types, which he called exposition, argument, faceting, categorising and analogy.

- With *exposition*, a preacher normally followed the order of the passage being used, explaining, interpreting and applying the words and phrases as the sermon proceeded. The sermon's structure was determined by the biblical text.

- In *faceting*, a preacher set before the congregation the different aspects of the topic, like a jeweller cutting a precious stone to show it in its best light.

- With *categorising*, the preacher arranged the sermon contents in categories or lists which then became the sermon's structure.

- Using *argument*, the structure followed point by point the logic of the case being made.

- In *analogy*, the preacher developed the theme by comparing it to something else, often from everyday life, and that comparison itself provided the structure.

Though I respect the late Dr Sangster's great skills as both preacher and teacher, I am not altogether happy with his use of the phrase *structural types*. Intellectually his analysis appeals to my desire for orderliness, tidiness, and good management, but if it is applied too rigorously it can cause problems. There are no off the peg patterns to which sermons conform, there are clear overlaps between them, and there are other structural patterns such as those of storytelling and bridge-building. Moreover, preachers sometimes employ more than one structural pattern in the same sermon.

Rather than thinking of structural types, which may

suggest an unhelpful rigidity, it is better to treat them as *structural skills,* those techniques, tools or even devices employed as appropriate in a sermon's structure. Sometimes we shall find ourselves using just one of these skills in a sermon. At other times we may wish to employ a variety of structural skills in one sermon. Whatever skills we use, however, it is important to ensure that our sermon has a basic structural unity. Where that unity is lacking, there is a strong possibility that we may be trying to preach two or more sermons at the same time. Frequent reminders of the aim help to remedy this.

STRUCTURAL VARIETY

As our experience of preaching grows, we do well to remind ourselves of the need for structural variety, for using the same structure every time will bore both us and those who hear us frequently. The thriller writers' art of taking people by surprise is also a useful one for preachers to cultivate.

A respected traditional structure is the so-called 'three-decker' sermon, consisting of three main points or sections sandwiched between an introduction and a conclusion. This was the pattern required of students for theological degrees in medieval universities, who were expected to preach three-point sermons on biblical texts as part of their examinations. Despite the parodying to which such sermons have been subjected over the years – 'I tell them what I'm going to say, then I say it, and then I tell them what I've said' – this well-tried model still has its place. Some sermon materials seem to fall naturally into a threefold pattern, and there is little wrong with that if it seems appropriate, though few contemporary preachers would argue, as some of their predecessors did, that it derives its threefold form from belief in God as trinity.

When a three-point sermon structure becomes an inflexible habit, however, the time has come for the mould to be broken, or at least set aside for a time. When as a curate I began to preach, members of my congregation good-humouredly asked why my sermons always had three points. I had to learn that not every sermon needs three, that sometimes two will do, and that at other times more than three will be needed. Whether a sermon has one, two, three, or more points, however, is secondary. What matters is the reliability and effectiveness of a building's structural form, not the number of pieces of scaffolding used to get it off the ground.

We all need to work hard to ring the changes in the way we organise sermon content. Whatever our personal preferences, we can add to our repertoire. Skilled expositors, for example, may sometimes use categorising or faceting; those who habitually use analogy may occasionally employ argument; and born storytellers can temper this with some bridge-building sermons which relate Bible narrative to contemporary culture.

STRUCTURING IN PRACTICE

It may be helpful to work through preparation stages from the choice of a theme to the designing of a structure, using the following examples.

EXAMPLE ONE

Let us suppose that our Bible passage is Luke 9:18–27 and our theme is discipleship. We have worked through the essential preliminaries mentioned earlier, noting that for this particular occasion the congregation will probably consist of about sixty regular worshippers, most of whom have a Christian background, but complemented by an expected sprinkling of visitors about whose Christian background we know nothing. Ages range from thirty to seventy. Many are employed, a few have retired. The employed are mainly professional people, including a couple of local medical doctors, a handful of teachers, and a solicitor.

We have worked hard at the Bible passage with the help of commentaries and have also allowed our minds to range freely over other resource materials, making notes as we have proceeded. The twenty minutes allotted to the sermon will not allow time to expound the whole of this fascinating and challenging passage, so we begin to focus on verse 23:

> Jesus said, 'If any want to become my followers, let them deny themselves, and take up their cross daily and follow me.'

Aware of the need for a definite aim, we have asked ourselves which particular aspect of discipleship will be specific, appropriate, and, as far as possible, achievable on this occasion. Our first effort was: *to show what Christ requires of his disciples*. Then, as we thought again of the professionals in the congregation, we decided to rephrase it more imaginatively as *to examine Christ's job description for his disciples*.

Having completed all these earlier stages of preparation, we are now ready to think about structure, a suitable framework, outline, or skeleton around which we can build our sermon to achieve our aim. Some of our congregation will be very familiar with job descriptions and we wish to latch on to their experience, so we decide to use that experience in our sermon. Job descriptions always say something about the person required and the job to be done. So, using our Bible passage, we draft our structure in the form of questions and answers about a job description for Christian disciples as follows:

1. *What kind of people are required?*
   a) Those who believe in their Employer! – a reference to the Caesarea Philippi incident which provides the context of verse 23.
   b) Those who are willing to learn, for that is the meaning of 'disciple'.

2. *What does the job entail?*
   a) Unselfishness – renouncing self.
   b) Cross-bearing – the forms this may take.
   c) Perseverance – 'day after day'.

Consider some of the skills used in planning this structure:

- *Exposition* – Our framework has grown from, and will lead yet further into, some straightforward biblical exposition, with the reference to the Caesarea Philippi context, an explanation of the word 'disciple', and the references to self-renunciation, cross-bearing, and perseverance found in the text.

- *Categorising* – In addition to exposition, in which we have followed the textual order, a traditional characteristic of much expository preaching, we have also picked up our categorising tool, for each of the questions is followed by answers in the form of two lists.

- *Analogy* – In the background of all of this is another structuring skill, for without labouring the point we have been using the analogy of a secular job description to highlight the kind of people required to be disciples and the type of work they are called to do.

EXAMPLE TWO

Aiming to show the immensity of Christ's love, we might use a paraphrase of Ephesians 3:18:

> May you, in company with all God's people, be strong to grasp what is the breadth and length and height and depth of Christ's love, and to know it, though it is beyond knowledge.

We could have decided to preach a straightforward expository sermon, working through the text phrase by phrase in the biblical order, explaining, interpreting, and applying scripture as the sermon proceeded.

Instead, we decide to call the sermon *Aspects of Love* and decide that we need a structure enabling us to focus on the distinctively Christian meaning of love before going on to deal with the four facets of God's love mentioned in the passage. After trying several rough drafts, we decide that the following framework best suits our purpose:

1. *The nature of God's love:*
   The implications of the word 'agape' – God's unconditional love.

2. *The extent of God's love:*
   a) Its breadth
   b) Its length
   c) Its height
   d) Its depth

Lancelot Andrewes, the great seventeenth-century preacher, was a skilled exponent of this kind of preaching. Archbishop Tillotson, himself a great seventeenth-century preacher, said of Andrewes, 'He cuts and polishes a text, like a jeweller a diamond, and the rays of truth from its heart of light flash from every facet.'[62] In the above example, we have used the skill of *faceting*, for love has become a four-faceted jewel shown to the congregation in such a way that these aspects of God's love sparkle before the congregation. The sermon, however, is not exclusively an example of faceting, for it begins with *exposition*, drawing the congregation's attention to what the Bible means by love.

EXAMPLE THREE

On another occasion, if we were preaching on Psalm 139:7–12 and aiming to show that God is with us everywhere, we might use the following framework.

1. *God is with you whatever your spiritual state*
   a) In the heights of heaven
   b) In the depths of the grave

2. *God is with you wherever you are*
   a) As far as you can go east
   b) As far as you can go west

3. *God is with you whatever your circumstances*
   a) In darkness
   b) In light

This structure involves the use of *categorising,* note the lists, and *exposition,* for we should need to explain, interpret and apply the biblical text. It provides another example of the use of more than one of the structuring skills in the same sermon.

---

[62] Cited in Charles Smyth, *The Art of Preaching*, p.123.

EXAMPLE FOUR

A sermon whose aim is to point to the characteristics of Christian love shown in 1 Corinthians 13 lends itself mainly to a *categorising* structure. Our skeleton might consist of two lists showing what love is not and what it is.

Love is *not:*	Love *is:*
a) envious;	a) patient;
b) boastful;	b) kind;
c) conceited;	c) courteous;
d) touchy;	d) unselfish;
e) unforgiving;	e) strong;
f) judgmental.	f) limitless.

Once again, however, it is difficult to see how we could properly handle 1 Corinthians 13 without also using *expositional* skills. Equally, there might be an overlap here between *categorising* and *faceting*, for especially in the second half of the sermon we shall be turning the jewel of love round so that some of its aspects (patience, kindness, etc.) might sparkle before the congregation.

EXAMPLE FIVE

Surprising his hearers with the unexpected twist at the end of his sermon topic, 'The Pain of *Answered* Prayer,' one experienced preacher used a sophisticated form of the skill of argument, proceeding as follows:

When you ask for God's guidance you sometimes hear things you'd rather not.

    a)   Isn't that a biblical experience?
    b)   Isn't that other people's experience?
    c)   Isn't that your experience?

What does this say about prayer for God's guidance?
   a)   Prayer may be dangerous to your comfort.
   b)   Prayer may be dangerous to your security.
   c)   Prayer may be dangerous to your ambition.

Can anything be said on the other side?
   Yes – that all progress is progress in God's light.[63]

Though the main thrust of that sermon depends on the skilful use of *argument*, this preacher was also using *expositional* and *categorising* skills.

There are a number of examples of analogy in the teaching of Jesus, especially in the discourses arising out of the seven 'I ams' in St John's Gospel.[64]

- Life-supporting bread provides an analogy of Christ as 'the Bread of Life'.

- Light dispelling darkness points to Christ as 'the Light of the World'.

- The entrance to the sheepfold points to Christ as 'the door' into his fold.

- The faithful shepherd points to Christ as 'the Good Shepherd'.

- Raising Lazarus provides an analogy of Christ as 'resurrection and life'.

- Thomas' question about the way becomes an opportunity for Christ to point to himself as 'the Way, the Truth and the Life'.

- The picture of a vine with its branches shows Christ as 'the true vine' on whom his followers as 'branches' all depend.

---

[63] Sangster, op. cit., p.76ff.
[64] Gospel according to St John 6:35, 8:12, 10:7, 10:11, 11:25, 14:6, 15:1.

In this kind of preaching, the comparison, often made point by point, provides the sermon framework and may also be a way into what to some are difficult Bible passages. Here are two examples.

EXAMPLE SIX

Using a popular television programme as a way in to Colossians 3:1–17, and aiming to show how Christ wants to change our lives, my theme at a family service was *A Christian Makeover* and my aim was *to show how Christ can transform us.* For the benefit of those who were unaware of such programmes, I explained that 'makeovers' were those entertaining, some would say, appalling, TV transformations of ordinary individuals into people with alleged class and flair. The pattern is always the same. The human guinea pigs appear dressed in their conventional way, and, I suspect, filmed from the worst possible angles. They are then handed over to the transformation team, the fashion, hairdressing, and make-up experts. After a time, the guinea pigs return to the studio to the audience's chorus of *ohs* and *ahs*. They have been transformed – 'made over'. They look younger, trendier, and much more attractive.

I then made the connection with Colossians 3:1–17.

St. Paul was in the '*Christian* make-over' business. He illustrated what he meant about the need for Christians to be transformed by talking about clothes – about taking off one set of clothes and putting on another. But the changes Paul wanted were not to do with appearance, but with fundamental changes of character. He wanted a 'makeover' which would transform behaviour. He said, 'Put on garments that suit God's chosen and beloved people.'

My sermon framework turned out as follows.

'Dirty clothes' to take off:	'Clean clothes' to put on:
fornication,	compassion,
indecency,	kindness,
lust,	humility,
evil desires,	gentleness,
filthy talk,	patience,
greed, rage,	tolerance,
bad temper,	forgiveness.
malice,	
slander, lies.	

As with the previous examples, the overlap with other structuring skills is obvious. Though the sermon is at heart an *analogy*, it also makes use of *categorising* by using the two lists. In addition, any attempt to give meaning to the contents of the lists requires some *exposition,* to bring out the biblical meaning of the vices and virtues mentioned.

EXAMPLE SEVEN

Using Hebrews 12, the London Marathon provided me with an analogy of discipleship as participation in a race. The marathon attracts thousands of participants, ranging from elite athletes to very ordinary men and women, and includes wheelchair competitors and blind people accompanied by guides. Spectators numbering hundreds of thousands lining the course, and millions more watching the run on television, witness many examples of incredible endurance and give their support to the competitors. Up to 98 per cent of the runners persevere, some for more than six hours, to complete the 26-mile course.

The analogy suggests several possible sermon outlines, but as my *aim was to show that the Christian race is a lifelong marathon* rather than a short sharp sprint, I decided on the following structure:

PREPARATION	PARTICIPATION	PERSEVERANCE
deciding	starting to run	effort
changing	running the course	encouragement
training	running with others	reward

Once more, however, this sermon is not exclusively *analogical*, for it also makes use of *categorising* in the subdivisions of its three main sections. Also, by using this framework, although I was able to latch onto something which is often given national media publicity, I did not deviate far from Hebrews, so there is an element of *exposition* to complement the analogy and the categorising.

You will notice that there is also some *alliteration*, the three main headings beginning with P. This sometimes works, but can be done to death. I recall preaching to a congregation of students training to be teachers a sermon based on Ephesians 5:1: *'Be imitators of God, as beloved children, and walk in love, as Christ loved us, and gave himself up for us'* (RSV). Too clever by half, my four headings were – Imitation, Filiation, Application and Inspiration. I just about got away with it – but it was touch and go!

Going back to analogies, the secret is not to press the comparison too far. If, like the author, you have taken part in marathons, you have to be on your guard against using this particular analogy too frequently or, when you do use it, of playing it to death! I served my second curacy with a brave man who, as Archdeacon of Tunis, worked with the Tunisian Resistance during the Second World War. Frequent use of those experiences in his preaching could be distracting, though they remained a topic of good-natured humour to the congregation.

CHECKLIST FIVE – STRUCTURES

In the light of your aim and collected resources, and bearing in mind the nature of your expected congregation:

- Try out a few possible structures for your sermon.

- Which structure is most likely to enable you to achieve your aim?

- Does it arise naturally out of the selected Bible passage, the chosen theme, and the collected resource materials?

- Is the structure dynamic rather than static, indicating how the sermon is to develop?

- Can the structure be set out as a series of short headings which make sense because they follow one another in an orderly way?

- Will these headings enable you to express clearly what you want to say?

- Is the structure a strong enough skeleton to take the 'flesh' with which it will need to be clothed?

- Does it provide a suitable framework around which to build an interesting sermon that will hold people's attention?

8. SCRIPTS

We have dealt with choice of theme, gathering of resources, clarification of aim, and design of structure. There remain two more overlapping tasks before the sermon is ready to be preached:

- Writing a first draft to put flesh on the sermon's skeleton and to provide an introduction, a conclusion, and illustrations where necessary;
- Checking through this draft and writing it up as the completed sermon script.

These are our concerns in this chapter.

FIRST DRAFT

As stated in the previous chapter, a strong and reliable structure is as vital to a sermon as a skeleton is to a body. By itself, however, it is insufficient, for the substance of each section needs to be drafted carefully to give the skeleton flesh.

Each section of the draft should have a strong start that will help to win and hold a congregation's attention, and a built-in unity that contributes to the sermon's single specific aim. It is also essential to use the spoken language of a sermon, rather than the written language of an essay or lecture. Throughout the draft attention needs to be given to what David Buttrick calls *'logical coherence; ideas must follow one another by some sort of connective logic'.*[65] Such clear links

---

[65] Buttrick, *Homiletic,* p.70.

between sections help to facilitate movement from one section to another. Without them a congregation may be given the impression that the sermon is a series of short, disconnected sections, each of which could easily have been a sermon in its own right. As Buttrick says, '*When we preach we speak in formed modules of language arranged in some patterned sequence.*'[66] Significantly in this context, Buttrick describes sermon sections as 'moves'.

The timing of each section, and therefore the effect it has on the sermon as a whole, needs to be given careful thought. Buttrick, an American, believes that each of a sermon's moves, or what British preachers have traditionally thought of as the sections or points of a sermon, should take about four minutes preaching time to explore and develop. On this basis, he argues that the optimum number of moves in a sermon is probably five. In a United Kingdom setting, particularly if we are preaching within a clearly defined liturgical context, we might have to settle for fewer sections or at least to spend less time developing them. If each section were to last up to four minutes, and with time added for the introduction and conclusion, a five-section sermon would take considerably longer than the fifteen to twenty minutes that most British congregations have come to expect.

DISCARDING WHAT IS UNNECESSARY

As we build up the body of the sermon section by section, we shall almost certainly find that we have more material than we can handle, or than is necessary to achieve our aim, and shall need to discard some of it. The willingness to discard is another important part of preparation, and we may well resist it. At that stage it may be of some comfort to remind ourselves

---

[66] Buttrick, p.23.

that we can save what we have discarded for use on another occasion. On this occasion, like the seventh-eighths lying beneath the surface of the iceberg, it has served as a useful basis for everything else. With every sermon, much more goes into the preparation than appears when it is complete.

ILLUSTRATIONS

A sermon without illustrations is like a house without windows, but as some houses indicate, 'windows' can be overdone. Some would say the only purpose of an illustration is to throw light on the point that the sermon is trying to make. Illustrations can, however, add interest and a lighter touch and this is all to the good if, at the same time, they clarify and illuminate.

Normally illustrations will be simple, brief, and to the point. They can be collected from a variety of sources such as newspapers and books, examples from life, lessons from history, the natural world, and other places. Illustrations should be allowed to speak for themselves, for like jokes they tend to fall flat if they have to be explained. They are not meant to be ends in themselves, or worse a collection of unconnected stories strung together to make sermons more entertaining. The test of any illustration is to ask whether it furthers the sermon's aim and throws light on the point that is being made.

Good stories and other illustrations should never be dropped into the text of a sermon without any real preparation. The way they are introduced, the language used, and the following pause to let the point sink in, are all important. To get the most out of illustrations, we need to prepare them as carefully as any other part of the sermon.

When using analogy, and especially when the analogy forms the structure around which the whole sermon is developed, time will be needed to develop the analogy, as was the case in the 'makeover' and 'marathon' sermons outlined in Chapter 7. Normally, however, illustrations are a small, though important, part of sermons and should be treated accordingly. Generally, they need be simple and straightforward in both content and expression, so that any member of a congregation may see the point they are illustrating. Illustrations should never be allowed to take over the sermon.

People remember illustrations long after they have forgotten everything else about a sermon and sometimes they are interested in an illustration without appreciating what it is illustrating. A few years ago I met someone who had heard me preach over twenty years earlier. 'I remember it well,' she told me. 'It was a family service and you preached about a sixpence.' Lulled into thinking this must have been one of my better sermons, I was duly impressed and asked how I had used the now redundant coin to illustrate the point I was making. 'I can't remember,' she replied, 'but I do remember you used a sixpence.'

VISUAL AIDS

Depending on the suitability of the building and the appropriateness of the occasion, we may wish to use audio-visual aids. This is especially useful when speaking to a group with a wide age range and of broad social background, as at a family service. The possibilities range from overhead projectors, flip charts and videos to a simple object held in the hand. We must ensure, however, that whatever is used is of a high standard, that people can see or hear it, and that it contributes to our aim. Otherwise it defeats its purpose and can be very frustrating to the congregation.

CONCLUSION

Although there may be very good reasons why Paul appears to have decided at first to end his letter to the Philippians at Chapter 3 verse 1, but then went on for another two chapters before stopping, this should not be regarded as a good precedent for preachers. When we say 'finally', people are expecting us to stop, and we should not disappoint them. We need to know when and how to finish.

This raises the question of how long a sermon should last. The answer depends on the occasion, the congregation, the local tradition, and who is preaching. A small congregation at an early morning service is unlikely to welcome a sermon lasting more than eight to ten minutes. A mixed congregation at a family service is likely to be happy with a longer sermon, provided we aim to say something relevant to young people as well as adults, involve the children in some way, and perhaps use visual aids. A well-established church, where there is a tradition of good preaching, will probably look forward to a longer sermon. Much depends upon the quality of the preaching. When some people preach for five minutes it seems like twenty; and when others end after fifteen minutes, we wish they had continued. Even when we think we possess the oratory of someone like Winston Churchill, we do well to remember that even he was realistic enough to admit, 'The head cannot take in more than the seat can endure.'

Having decided how long our sermon should last, we need to think carefully about how we may best bring it to a successful end? As with every other part of a sermon, the answer lies in careful preparation. Conclusions do not just happen. They need to be planned. Lord Mancroft is reputed to have said, 'A speech is like a love affair. Any fool can start it, but to end it requires considerable skill.'

The conclusion should round off the sermon in such a way that the congregation knows where we have been taking them, what we are now expecting of them, and that we really have finished. There should be only one conclusion. At this stage of the sermon, we should not introduce new ideas, except to whet the congregation's appetite for other occasions as, for example, when the sermon is one of a series. Our conclusion needs to be brief, simple, positive and direct, leaving the congregation asking how they need to respond to what has been said.

INTRODUCTION

Sometimes an introduction may suggest itself at the beginning of sermon preparation. This is good, as long as the suggestion fits in with the aim and does not dictate the development of the rest of the sermon. Often the planning of the introduction will come at the end of sermon preparation, for then we are more fully aware of what it is we wish to introduce.

We should remember that the fivefold purpose of the introduction is:

- to win attention,
- to stimulate interest,
- to indicate something of what is to follow,
- to encourage the congregation's confidence in the preacher,
- and to establish a sense of shared purpose between preacher and hearers.

To fulfil this purpose, the introduction, which should be as short as possible, needs to be as well prepared as any other part of the sermon.

Though there may be preachers who, with a vague idea in mind, will produce a snappy introduction before they have formed a sermon, their products are usually a problem. Like a dud Roman candle, their sermons may flash brightly at the start and then, often, fizzle out.[67]

Some have suggested that, to whet the appetite for what is to follow, the longest pause in the sermon's delivery should usually come immediately after the introduction.[68]

FINAL SCRIPT

Opinions differ about whether preachers should write out their sermons in full, and whether they should use full manuscripts or brief notes when preaching. We all learn from experience what is best for us. Writing a full script is especially helpful for inexperienced preachers. Those faced with a fairly rigid time slot for the sermon will also find that it helps us to use the available time in the best way.

Some people suggest there is something not quite Christian about writing out a sermon in full. They claim that if preachers believe God has given them a message, they should rely on Him to enable them to preach it without preparing a full script. They sometimes quote Matthew 10:19–20 to support their view, pointing out that when sending out the Twelve, Jesus told them, 'Do not worry about what you are to say; when the time comes, the words you need will be given you; for it is not you who will be speaking: it will be the Spirit of your Father speaking in you.' Had they referred to the context of this quotation, they would have been hard-pressed to use it to support their view, for Jesus was instructing the Twelve how they should act when

---

[67] Buttrick, p.83.
[68] Buttrick, p.87.

they were arrested.

David Sheppard tells the story of Archbishop Frederick Temple's unexpected visit to one of his parishes where he heard an unscripted and ill-prepared sermon. Afterwards the preacher explained, 'Your Grace, I took a vow that I would always speak without notes.' Having heard the sermon, the archbishop solemnly pronounced that he freed the preacher from his vow![69]

There are preachers who can memorise text so easily that having read a sermon script once they can repeat it almost word for word without looking at it again. Most preachers lack that ability and have to use a script or outline notes. They also learn from experience that what can be read easily at home is not always as visible at a lectern or from a pulpit.

Those using full scripts can take heart from Henry Emerson Fosdick:

> I always write out my sermon in full. To the best of my recollection, after nearly forty years of preaching, I have never preached a sermon that was not written out fully. I do not see how one can keep his substance serious, and his style flexible and varied unless he writes in full. At any rate, for myself there is no other method that is conceivable. As for delivery, that I can handle in various ways; sometimes having the manuscript before me and reading freely; and sometimes drawing an outline from it and speaking from the notes.[70]

Where does all of that leave what is called spontaneous or extempore preaching? Winston Churchill is widely recognised as one of the great twentieth-century orators. During his inspirational wartime speeches, what seemed spontaneous had usually been painstakingly prepared, written out in full with secretarial help, and very carefully

---

[69] Sheppard, *Steps Along Hope Street*, p.245.
[70] Cited in Prochnow, op. cit., p.5.

rehearsed, even down to the gestures and little hesitancies over certain words that characterised his broadcasts. As one of his admirers wrote:

> Winston Churchill's eloquence did not just happen. It was not accidental. It was the most carefully studied effort of a great mind that had struggled word by word and phrase by phrase for the brilliant expression of ideals that would move nations.[71]

THE LANGUAGE OF PREACHING

All public speakers have to remember that they are speaking, not reading an essay. Vivian Summers points out,

> The dullest speech is the one that sounds like a spoken essay. Artificial turns of phrase, faithful obedience to the rules of grammar and syntax. ... and finely honed prose have their place in written work but tend to sound stilted and unnatural in speech.[72]

Preachers need to learn that lesson, especially as in many cases our educational background is that which measured success through essay writing. A sermon script may look ideal on paper, but may turn out to be eminently unsuitable when preached. The crucial test is not whether the sermon script is written in polished English, but whether it communicates what we wish to say. Normally, a congregation will hear a sermon only once. Unlike those reading a book, they cannot look back over something they have not quite grasped the first time. Nor can they pause to use a dictionary to look up words they do not understand. The language of the sermon must never be over-sophisticated, or its meaning esoteric, otherwise the message will be obscured rather than made clear.

---

[71] Ibid., p.48.
[72] Vivian Summers, *Public Speaking*, p.49.

John Bell of the Iona Community is a good example of how to use the kind of language that will make preaching come alive. Ten examples of his distinctive and captivating preaching style in *Wrestle and Fight and Pray*,[73] show that Bell's sermons:

- are based on a theme arising from a set Bible reading;
- begin with an introduction that immediately wins attention;
- are written in simple sentences in down-to-earth, spoken language, designed to be heard rather than read;
- use repetition to emphasise the points he is making;
- contain good illustrations, many of them based on his personal experience;
- and make clear the relevance of what he is preaching to everyday life.

Writing the Introduction to Bell's book, Duncan Forrester acknowledges that the 'emotional surcharge' that once sustained a great succession of notable Scottish preachers is no longer evident. Yet the tradition of preaching, though changed, is still very much alive and well. 'Scottish preaching is still passionate, thoughtful, biblical, challenging, and deeply concerned with the relevance of the gospel to the needs of today's world.'[74] Nowhere is this more obvious than in John Bell's preaching. All who aspire to preach effectively will benefit from reading *Wrestle and Fight and Pray*.

---

[73] John L Bell, *Wrestle and Fight and Pray*.
[74] Ibid., p.vii f.

CHECKLIST SIX – THE SERMON SCRIPT

1. Does each section of your draft:

- start strongly?
- flow logically?
- have an inbuilt unity?
- end firmly?
- link up with what precedes and follows it?

2. Does your introduction:

- command attention?
- stimulate interest?
- prepare for what is to follow?
- encourage confidence in the preacher?
- help to establish a sense of shared purpose between preacher and hearers?

3. Do your illustrations:

- add interest?
- throw light on the point you are trying to make?
- speak for themselves and need no explanation?
- if they require presentation of visual material, are they big enough and clear enough to be seen by all?

4. Does your conclusion:

- indicate clearly (and briefly) that the sermon is ending?
- end positively?
- present a challenge and elicit a response?

9. PERFORMING

'There is no getting away from the fact that a public speaker is a performer, just as much as an actor or singer is,' writes Vivian Summers.[75] This chapter is written in the conviction that the same is true of preachers, who, you may think, are in a completely different category from other public speakers. You may wish to argue that preachers of God's Word are never really performing. That depends on what is meant by 'performing'. 'What a performance!' is something that may be said about a piece of aggressive, embarrassing, or unacceptable behaviour. Clearly, preaching is not that kind of performance. If, on the other hand, we mean a well-executed public presentation of a piece of work after many hours of careful preparation, then performing effectively is an apt description of what well-prepared preachers should be doing whenever they preach.

Musicians and broadcasters do their utmost through their sheer professionalism to ensure that their material is properly prepared, mastered, and rehearsed. Following their performances, they often review and assess what they have done, hoping to learn from their experiences so that they may be even more effective next time. Learning from them, preachers should aim to be as effective in their work, as these other public performers are in theirs. How may we, with well-prepared sermons, go on to perform effectively in the service of God?

First, we need to remind ourselves of some of those basic assumptions made in Chapter 1 about:

---

[75] Summers, op. cit., p.11.

- Our vocation – we believe God has called us to preach;
- Our commitment – we are fully dedicated to our task as ministers of God's Word;
- Our study – careful preparation has equipped us for the task;
- Our character – what we are is as important as what we say;
- Our spirituality – how we relate to God is of paramount importance as we seek to speak in his name. We have prayed for ourselves and our hearers that what we say may be a Word of God to them.

The rest of this chapter is concerned with the practicalities of the preaching we are about to do – the final steps needed to enable us to perform effectively. These concern final preparations, sermon presentation, and post-preaching assessment.

FINAL PREPARATIONS

Some kind of rehearsal is vital. Like one famous preacher, this may simply take the form of privately reading the sermon aloud. George MacLeod, founder of the Iona Community and a gifted preacher, 'went over and over his sermons – wearing out the carpet in Dunsmeorach, a family house near the Abbey owned by the Community. Every phrase, every pause, every gesture was rehearsed'. Little wonder that 'each MacLeod sermon was a Word-event, a happening, an experience which could both raise wild goose pimples and change lives'.[76] Ronald Ferguson tells us that George's aphorisms were not extempore but prepared and practised. MacLeod had at least one thing in common with another George, George Bernard Shaw, who is reputed to have said, 'I am the most spontaneous speaker in

---

[76] Ronald Ferguson, *George MacLeod, Founder of the Iona Community,* p.241.

the world, because every word, every gesture and every retort has been carefully rehearsed.'

After reading the script through several times to ensure that it has been mastered, it may be helpful to record ourselves preaching it. As we listen to the playback, we may find that parts of the sermon need to be rephrased to make it flow better, that what looked fine in print does not quite come across in speech, and we can time how long the sermon is likely to last.

SERMON PRESENTATION

An American researcher, Albert Mehrabian, claims that 55 per cent of a speaker's impact on hearers is visual, 38 per cent of the impact comes from the speaker's voice, and only 7 per cent comes from what the speaker says.[77] I am not aware of any similar research relating to preachers and their congregations. Most preachers would expect sermon content to count for more. Even if we allow for a large margin of error in Mehrabian's figures, however, they do suggest that the impact of a sermon may depend on the preacher's voice and appearance as well as upon the sermon content.

Writers about public speaking emphasise the importance of a speaker's posture and appearance. 'Your stance, your mannerisms, your movements – controlled or fidgety – all convey something about your personality and will affect your success as a public speaker,' wrote Vivian Summers.[78] 'Whatever you are wearing, do the audience the courtesy of making the best of your appearance. If you are careless of how you look, you are telling them that you do not think much of them.'[79] Preachers should always take care that their appearance does not get in the way of their message.

---

[77] Cited in Anne Nicholls, *How to Master Public Speaking,* p.100.
[78] Summers, op. cit., p.13.
[79] Ibid., p.81.

There is something to be said for preaching from a pulpit or a lectern, for they help to control a preacher's movements. With some over-mobile preachers such control can be a positive advantage. But there is no golden rule about this. Some preachers make their impact because of their mobility. Towards the end of a long and distinguished ministry, the ailing Aubrey Aitken, then Bishop of Lynn, had almost lost what had been a remarkable preaching voice. Not to be deterred, and attached with a long lead to an amplifier, he would wander up and down the aisle growling out his sermons. His congregation would listen, enraptured. Nobody who heard him would have missed it for the world.

Some people speak with their hands, and would feel totally inhibited if they tried to stop their gestures. Others wander about in front of a congregation, believing this can help those listening to them to feel more fully involved in the preaching experience. Provided we are sensitive enough to know when our mannerisms are getting in the way of the message, we should be ourselves. There is, however, one rule that applies to every preacher. We should try to *maintain eye contact* with the congregation, for this helps to engage them and to hold their attention.

Vivian Summers says, 'As a public speaker you are presenting not only your material but also your personality to the audience, and the chief vehicle of this is your voice.' She adds, 'Accept your own voice and train it to be as effective as you can make it.'[80] Many books have been written about voice production and in almost any part of the country there are people with training skills to help those with particular difficulties. If we have sung in a choir, we may have overcome the worst of these, and will have learnt something of the importance of breathing and clear enunciation. But here are some basic rules.

---

[80] Ibid., p.155f.

- We should present our material in a lively and interesting way. We may have the most wonderful sermon to preach, but performing it in a deadpan manner, never smiling, and with a take-it-or-leave-it attitude may make most of the congregation switch off long before they have stopped to hear whether we have anything to offer.

- We should look up and speak up. We should know the content of our sermon so well that we are not too tied to our script or notes, for as well as losing that vital eye contact mentioned earlier, we shall find our voice disappearing into the pulpit or lectern.

- We should speak clearly, audibly and without affectation. Like anybody else performing in public, we shall need to be careful of our diction, paying particular attention to our consonants and word endings. If we want our congregation to understand they should not steal, it is very important to make them hear the 'not' as well as the 'steal'! Listening to the playback of our recorded sermons can help us to correct any initial difficulties of this kind before they become habitual.

- We should try to vary our volume, tone, pitch and speed. Listening to speech of any kind can become tedious if speakers do not vary the manner of their presentation.

- We should aim to make good use of the pause. And when we pause, we should do it deliberately – and not for too long, or the congregation may think we have lost our place and become anxious on our behalf.

- If the church has an amplification system, we should learn what we can about its workings before the service.

- We should know when to stop. Important though preaching is, it has to fit into the rest of the service and has to be timed accordingly. It is better to end when the congregation wishes we would go on, than to continue long after its perseverance has worn thin. The effectiveness of a sermon is not to be judged by its length.

- When everything else has been said about preaching, being natural is perhaps as important as anything else. Advising someone wishing to succeed as a television presenter, Michael Palin, one of the ablest television communicators, gave as his three rules, 'One, be natural; two, be natural; three, be natural.'[81]

POST-PREACHING ASSESSMENT

At the end of a service, some members of a congregation may make polite remarks about the sermon. On occasions a hearer may wish to engage us in discussion about something we have said. As long as they go further than the traditional, 'Lovely sermon, vicar,' such responses can be valuable to help us reflect on our effectiveness. We can also be helped by the positive criticism of colleagues and husbands or wives. Perhaps the most searching kind of assessment, however, is likely to be self-assessment. We may find it helpful in this respect to use the self- assessment checklist at the end of this chapter.

---

[81] Interviewed on BBC on 25 October 1996.

POSTSCRIPT

Some readers may question the time required to follow the methods set out in this book, pointing to other time-consuming activities they face in Christian ministry. This is a problem faced by all Christians, but most of them are not called to preach. If we believe God has called us to a specific ministry of his Word, however, we shall have to allow some of these other aspects of ministry to be done by those not called to preach. We need to give our preaching preparation the priority it requires by managing our time appropriately.

There will be occasions when what we have prepared carefully is overtaken by events. If, for example, we find ourselves due to preach after a major national disaster, or an act of terrorism, or a tragedy affecting our local community, we may have to abandon a carefully prepared sermon because we judge it to be inappropriate in the light of what has happened. With little opportunity to prepare an alternative, we may have to settle for a sermon in which we speak more spontaneously, highlighting the disturbing event, making a brief Christian response to it, and following this with an extended period of silence and prayer.

None of this undermines the necessity for careful preparation to preach. It is a timely reminder, however, that when preachers have done all they can to prepare conscientiously for their work, they cannot prepare for the unexpected. Even when as preachers we believe we are fully prepared to preach effectively, and nothing unusual happens to alter arrangements, we still need to leave the outcome of our preaching with God, resting in the assurance of the Lord's words through Isaiah.

As the rain and the snow come down from heaven
and do not return there until they have watered the earth,
making it bring forth and sprout,
giving seed to the sower and bread to the eater,
so shall my word be that goes out from my mouth;
it shall not return to me empty,
but it shall accomplish that which I purpose,
and succeed in the thing for which I sent it.[82]

We have to prepare as if our effectiveness depends entirely on us, but to preach knowing that the outcome depends always on God.

---

[82] Isaiah 55:10f.

CHECKLIST SEVEN – SELF-ASSESSMENT

- Did the sermon achieve its aim?
- How effective were the introduction and conclusion?
- How successful was the sermon's structure?
- Did the sections of the sermon proceed in an ordered sequence, hang together, and develop the theme as intended?
- Was each part of the sermon necessary?
- How effective were the illustrations?
- Were the contents, style and language appropriate on this occasion to this congregation?
- What can you learn from this experience that will help you next time you preach?

BIBLIOGRAPHY

All Bible references are from the *New Revised Standard Version* (NRSV), except where shown differently.

Bell, John L, *Wrestle and Fight and Pray*, Saint Andrew Press, Edinburgh, 2003

Blackwood, Andrew, *The Preparation of Sermons*, Church Book Room Press, 1951

Briers, Richard, *Natter, Natter,* J M Dent & Sons Ltd., 1981

Buttrick, David, *Homiletic: Moves and Structures*, SCM Press Ltd., 1987

Dovan, G H, *Jowett the Preacher: His Life and Work,* New York, 1918

Ferguson, Ronald, *George MacLeod, Founder of the Iona Community*, HarperCollins, 1990

Ford, Cleverly, *Preaching Today*, Epworth and SPCK, 1969

Gunton, Colin, *Theology Through Preaching*, T & T Clark, 2001

Henderson, Noel, *The Goulburn Norwich Diaries*, Canterbury Press, 1996

Humphreys, John, *Lost for Words*, Hodder and Stoughton, 2004

Ireson, Gordon, *How Shall They Hear?*, SPCK, 1957

McGrath, Alister, *Bridge Building*, IVP, 2000

Nicholls, Anne, *How to Master Public Speaking*, How to Master Books Limited, 1993

Prior, John (Chairman, the Archbishops' Report), *Faith in the Countryside*, Churchman Publishing, 1990

Prochnow, Herbert, *Public Speakers Treasure Chest*, Thomas & Co., 1965

Sangster, W E, *The Craft of Sermon Construction*, Epworth Press, 1951

Sheppard, David, *Steps Along Hope Street*, Hodder & Stoughton, 2002

Smyth, Charles, *The Art of Preaching: 947–1939*, SPCK, 1940

Stott, John, *I Believe in Preaching*, Hodder & Stoughton, 1982

Summers, Vivian, *Public Speaking*, Penguin Books, London, 1988

Williams, Rowan, *Open To Judgement,* Darton, Longman and Todd 2002

Printed in the United Kingdom
by Lightning Source UK Ltd.
112858UKS00001B/85